THE
DARKEST
DAY

THE
DARKEST
DAY

The Washington-Baltimore Campaign During the War of 1812

CHARLES G. MULLER

UNIVERSITY OF PENNSYLVANIA PRESS

Philadelphia

Originally published 1963 as *The Darkest Day: 1814: The Washington-Baltimore Campaign* by J.B. Lippincott Company
Published by arrangement with HarperCollins Publishers, Inc.
Copyright © 1963 Charles G. Muller

Printed in the United States of America on acid-free paper

10 9 8 7 6 5 4 3 2 1

Published 2003 by
University of Pennsylvania Press
Philadelphia, Pennsylvania 19104-4011

Library of Congress Cataloging-in-Publication Data

Muller, Charles Geogffrey, 1897–
    The darkest day : the Washington-Baltimore campaign during the War of
1812 / Charles G. Muller.
        p.   cm.
    Originally published: Philadelphia : Lippincott, 1963.
    Includes bibliographical references and index.
    ISBN 0-8122-1843-4 (pbk. : alk. paper)
    1. United States—History—War of 1812—Campaigns. 2. Bladensburg,
Battle of, 1814. 3. Washington (D.C.)—History—Capture by the British,
1814. 4. Baltimore, Battle of, 1814. I. Title.
E355.6 .M8   2003
973.5'23—dc21   2002072129

Maps drawn by John Carnes

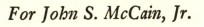

For John S. McCain, Jr.

CONTENTS

MAPS

1

WAR: 18 JUNE 1812

I

At the start of the War of 1812 against Great Britain, newspapers called it Mr. Madison's War. At the finish, histories called it America's Second War of Independence.

It began, 18 June 1812, to a nationwide clamor of political discontent. In Maryland, opponents likened President James Madison's administration to the street in Baltimore called by his name "which began at the poorhouse, went by the jail, then passed the penitentiary, and ended on Gallow's Hill."

Federalists, who upheld a central government independent of local government, had lost power to Republicans, who held that the states could remedy central government oppression by nullifying any obnoxious act. Nationalization hardly existed. Minorities used secession as a club to beat opponents to terms on important questions, and both sides—too often and on relatively insignificant matters—thought of breaking up the union.

Since the end of their first war with Great Britain, these United States of America—now eighteen, with Vermont, Kentucky, Tennessee, Ohio, and Louisiana—had suffered increasing indignities. Britain had issued Orders in Council which made American ships a prey for the British navy on the high seas; and from Milan Napoleon had proclaimed that France would look on neutral vessels subjecting themselves to search by British cruisers as lawful prizes of French frigates and privateers.

Madison inherited this problem from Thomas Jefferson and, like both Federalists and Republicans, looked on France as the lesser of the two evils. Under John Adams, the United States had fought France from 1797 to 1800 in a half—or sea—war that served as excuse for much raiding of merchant shipping and ended in peace with Napoleon, who had become First Consul.

To cope with England now, Madison had five alternatives:

1. Do nothing . . . let individual shipowners shift for themselves,
2. Try further negotiation,
3. Suspend all commerce with other nations,
4. Grant letters of marque and reprisal to American shipowners,
5. Declare war on Great Britain.

American temperament precluded doing nothing. Negotiation, ending with an 1806 treaty which Jefferson would not send to the Senate, had failed. Embargo, dutifully tried, had ended in repeal—with an accompanying resolution favoring defense of maritime rights against all belligerents. Which left only alternatives 4 and 5 as the situation deteriorated.

Congress voted continuance of non-intercourse with Great Britain; Great Britain continued her attempts to recover her commerce and take back her seamen. On 29 November 1811 Speaker of the House Henry Clay and John C. Calhoun of the Committee on Foreign Affairs, younger and more impetuous than earlier leaders, backed a resolution declaring that "forebearance has ceased to be a virtue. . . . The period has arrived when in the opinion of your committee it is the sacred duty of Congress to call forth the resources and patriotism of the country."

The committee favored increasing the standing Army of some 3,000 effectives by 10,000 men and authorizing the President to call 50,000 volunteers under arms. An overwhelming majority acceded, quickly. But without Madison's support, the resolution had no force. And the President wanted peace.

But with an election coming up, leaders who counseled action waited on Madison and laid the facts in his lap. They would support him for a second term if he accepted their war policy. With James Monroe and Elbridge Gerry ready, able, and willing to run on this policy, Madison accepted.

On 1 April 1812 he sent to Congress a recommendation for a 60-day embargo, and he wrote Jefferson that Great Britain's refusal to repeal her Orders in Council had left the United States no option but to prepare for war. Although Republicans and Federalists alike had gone along with Jefferson's desire to maintain neutrality and peace, a faction of the body politic always had favored a war with Great Britain. This faction provided the current nucleus for direct action.

On 1 June the President sent to Congress a message pointing out that the conduct of Great Britain presented a series of acts hostile to the United States as an independent and neutral nation:

"British cruisers have been in the continued practice of violating the American flag on the great highway of nations, and of seizing and carrying off persons sailing on it . . . thousands of American citizens, under the safeguard of public law and of their national flag, have been torn from their country and from everything dear to them; have been dragged on board ships-of-war of a foreign nation and exposed, under the severities of their discipline, to be exiled to the most distant and deadly climes, to risk their lives in the battles of their oppressors, and to be the melancholy instruments of taking away those of their own brethren. . . .

"British cruisers have been in the practice also of violating the rights and the peace of our coasts. They hover over and harass our entering and departing commerce. To the most

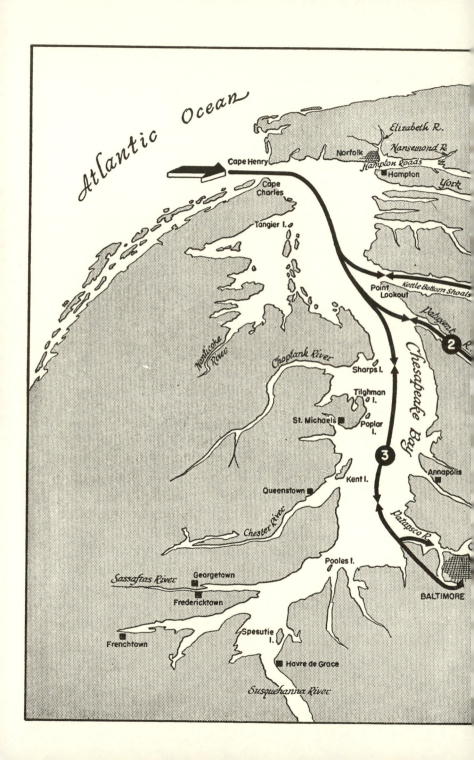

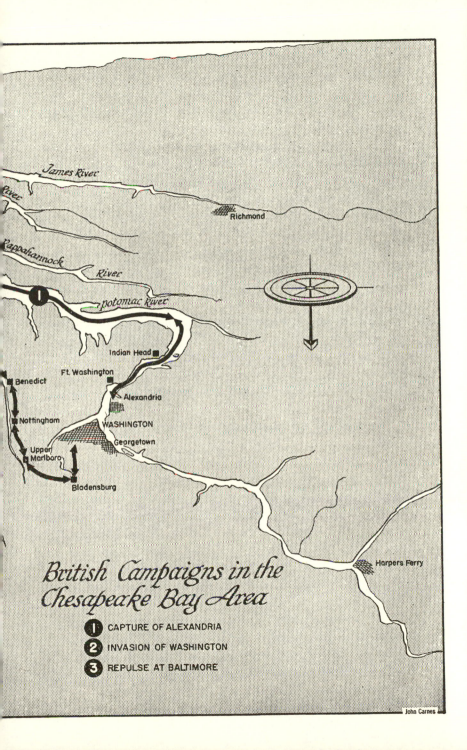

James River

Richmond

Rappahannock River

River

potomac river

Indian Head

Ft. Washington

Benedict

Alexandria

Nottingham

WASHINGTON

Upper Marlboro

Georgetown

Bladensburg

Harpers Ferry

British Campaigns in the Chesapeake Bay Area

1 CAPTURE OF ALEXANDRIA

2 INVASION OF WASHINGTON

3 REPULSE AT BALTIMORE

John Carnes

insulting pretensions they have added the most lawless proceedings in our very harbors, and have wantonly spilled American blood within the sanctuary of our territorial jurisdiction. . . .

"Under pretended blockades, without presence of an adequate force and sometimes without the practicability of applying one, our commerce has been plundered in every sea."

Madison recommended war.

He picked a propitious moment. For Napoleon, having taken over many of Europe's independent states as allies and vassals, kept Britain's soldiers busy on the Spanish peninsula in an effort to contain him—and kept her sailors busy in eastern Atlantic and Mediterranean waters in an effort to maintain her commerce with the Continent.

Now Napoleon invaded Russia, with the aim of excluding Britain's ships and goods from Arctic and Baltic ports. His war against the Emperor of Russia therefore constituted a war against the King of England. Under the circumstances, Britain would find it difficult to detach ships and soldiers to fight the United States.

The House of Representatives concurred, 79 to 49, in Madison's recommendation to go to war: in support, members from Vermont, some from New York, all but one from Pennsylvania, most of those from Maryland, Virginia and North Carolina, and all from South Carolina, Georgia, Kentucky, Tennessee, Ohio and Louisiana; in opposition, members from New Hampshire, most of those from Massachusetts, those from Connecticut, Rhode Island, New Jersey and Delaware, with several from New York, some from Virginia and North Carolina, one from Pennsylvania, and three from Maryland.

After two weeks of deliberation the Senate concurred, 19 to 13, with two senators not voting and Louisiana's not yet qualified: in support, senators from Vermont, Pennsylvania, Virginia, North Carolina, South Carolina, Georgia, Kentucky, Tennessee, and Ohio; in opposition, senators from New

Hampshire, Connecticut, Rhode Island, New York, and Delaware; divided, senators from Massachusetts, Maryland, and New Jersey.

Public opinion also split: on one side stood the instinctively patriotic young men of the country who enthusiastically greeted an offensive war voluntarily undertaken to compel Great Britain to respect the nation's maritime rights as a neutral; against them stood a portion of the community which conceded sufficient cause for direct action, but condemned Mr. Madison's War because of the time and mode of its declaration.

Madison thus faced a major problem—consolidating the union for war against an oppressor who saw this dissension and believed that Americans would not act as a united people either on the seas or in the homeland so recently freed from British dominion.

Representative Nathaniel Macon of North Carolina earlier had voiced the danger that lay in discord among the states: "I hope this to be no party war, but a national war. . . . Such a war, if war we shall have, can alone, in my judgment, obtain the end for which we mean to contend, without any disgrace."

And Daniel Webster of New Hampshire later re-emphasized that party support could not sustain the country through a long, expensive, and bloody contest. The cause, to be successful, he said "must draw to itself the sober approbation of the great mass of the people. It must enlist, not their temporary or party feelings, but their steady patriotism and their constant zeal.

"Unlike the old nations of Europe," he pointed out, with pardonable patriotism, "there are in this country no dregs of population fit only to supply the constant waste of war and out of which an army can be raised for hire at any time and for any purpose. Armies of any magnitude can be here nothing but the people embodied; and if the object be one for which the people will not embody there can be no armies."

It took the country as a whole a long time to appreciate this truth. America would suffer even greater indignities than Great Britain already had heaped upon her—the nation's capital sacked and burned—before her people came together without partisanship, without sectionalism, to achieve a victory that consolidated eighteen previously un-United States.

2

EARLY IN 1812 Congress had evolved a plan to carry all costs of an anticipated war of three years by loans, and in March had authorized, for the first year's expenses, a loan of $11 million at annual interest not to exceed 6 per cent and reimbursable in twelve years. By the time Congress declared war little more than half the needed money had come forth.

Not until eight days *after* the declaration of war did Congress take measures to consolidate the Army of the United States with new levies. It then aimed for a regular force of twenty regiments of foot, four of artillery, two of dragoons, and one of riflemen. With engineers and artificers, this force totaled 36,700 men on paper. But at the war's start the nation had in the ranks about 3,000 effectives only. As the year went on the regular Army force reached a top of 6,744.

For militia, Secretary of War William Eustis in April had written state governors:

"I am instructed by the President of the United States to call upon the executives of the different states to take effective measures to organize, arm, and equip, according to law, and hold in readiness, to march at a moment's warning, their respective portion of 100,000 militia, officers included. . . ."

Every community had its 1) standing, or drafted, militia—the town's able-bodied males, each with his own gun—assembling once or twice a year for muster, wasting no unnecessary time in drill, expecting to fight only if called up in an emergency.

Supplementing this standing militia, men who liked companionship and social approval formed 2) volunteer militia companies. These citizen soldiers, eager for battle action and glory, outfitted themselves in splendid uniforms, drilled weekly, paraded frequently, and brought an invaluable *esprit de corps* to the national military service. Most communities had one such volunteer militia unit, many towns took pride in more than one, and some cities enrolled enough companies to form regiments.

By law, however, no militia unit could be compelled to serve beyond the bounds of its own state and, when the standing militia did go out to fight, its commanding general's chief military problem usually arose from the fact that the men insisted on doing as they pleased on the battlefield—as on the drill field—fighting or not fighting as they saw fit.

Guarding the country against invasion, upwards of thirty forts (some unfinished) were spread over strategic terrain—from Fort Sumner in Maine south to Forts Pinckney, Moultrie, and Mechanic in South Carolina, and west along the Great Lakes to Fort Dearborn at Chicago.

With a theoretical half-million citizen soldiers available (more than Canada's entire civilian population of 400,000), the United States set out to invade Canada against 40,000 Canadian militia and 6,000 British troops. But no American general ever had 10,000 men fit for action at any one time and place, and the invasion foundered.

What with recalcitrant militia refusing flatly to enter Canada, with suspected treachery in high ranks, and with obvious ineptitude on the part of generals who have gone down in history as antiquated museum pieces, America's red-faced leaders ignominiously ended 1812 by resting defensively along the entire northern border.

At sea, where prospects had looked very bad for the United States, results proved very good.

The Navy floated three 44-gun frigates, four 36-gun frigates, three 32-gun frigates, ten smaller vessels of war, and 170 gunboats. The fleet assembled an aggregate of some 500 guns.

With these 500 *guns*, America sailed out against 1,042 British *ships!*

As mistress of the seas Great Britain boasted 254 ships-of-the-line with 74 guns and upwards; augmented by 35 lesser-powered ships, 247 frigates, and 506 smaller vessels of war.

David did not have to pit his slingshot against Goliath's full strength, however. Great Britain had first to spread her flotilla against France over the eastern Atlantic Ocean and across the Baltic, North, and Mediterranean Seas; after that she could concentrate on America in the western Atlantic.

So United States naval captains bearded the British lion on the high seas, picking their opportunities so well and concluding their work so successfully that within a year the lion screamed in London's press that England's maritime supremacy was being stripped from her "by a piece of striped bunting flying at the mastheads of a few fir-built frigates, manned by a handful of bastards and cowards."

Those words did not sit well, and Yankee privateers skippered and sailed by just such crews swarmed over the Atlantic to lend the Navy a hand. Estimates for the last six months of 1812 gave American sea forces a total of 250 merchantmen and more than 50 armed British vessels captured, with more than 3,000 prisoners taken.

Re-elected in 1812, Madison at his second inauguration, clearly voiced growing general sentiment:

"Our nation is, in number, more than half that of the British Isles. It is composed of a brave, a free, a virtuous and an intelligent people . . . the patriotism, the good sense and the manly spirit of our fellow citizens are pledges for the cheerfulness with which they will bear each his share of the common burthen.

"To render the war short, and its success sure, animated and systematic exertions alone are necessary; and the success of our arms now, may long preserve our country from the necessity of another resort to them."

But the President's optimistic prophecy lost conviction as

it echoed down the Potomac River to Chesapeake Bay. For at Christmas time Great Britain officially had declared a naval blockade of Delaware and Chesapeake Bays and, anticipating invasion of American waters, Acting Secretary of War James Monroe* had recommended to the chairman of the military committee in Congress:

"To make this war effectual, as to its just objects, so much of the physical force of the country must be brought into activity as will be adequate. The force exists in an abundant degree, and it is only necessary to call it forth and make a proper use of it. . . .

"The force will constitute the nucleus of a little army, to be formed, in case of invasion, of the militia, volunteers, or such other local force as may be specially organized. To be apportioned over six points along the coast . . . so the nation's regular force may be employed in offensive operations elsewhere."

James Monroe, 55 years old in 1813, had vigor, enthusiasm, and determination to go with a full head of curling white hair. A patriot who craved action, at 19 he had served as captain with General George Washington's army. Wounded at Trenton, he had fought at the Brandywine and at Germantown, and had become a major. A scout for Washington in the Battle of Monmouth, he also had served as an adjutant general.

An inveterate traveler on stage, packet, and horseback, he had ridden up and down the Eastern seaboard while a member of Congress and twice visited Indian country via the Great Lakes and "through the wilderness."

Besides having more military experience than any other Cabinet member, Colonel James Monroe probably had more personal knowledge of national topography. He proposed to

* War Secretary Eustis, blamed for early military disasters, dropped from Cabinet—along with Navy Secretary Paul Hamilton—effective 31 December 1812. Secretary of State James Monroe for some weeks before and after that date acted in dual role for State and War. On 5 February 1813, Brigadier-General John Armstrong took over War portfolio; on 12 January 1813, William Jones had taken over Navy portfolio.

defend the Chesapeake, in the manner he recommended to Congress, at Norfolk (in Virginia, at the bay's mouth) and at Annapolis (in Maryland, within the bay).

He explained:

"It may be said that it is not probable that the enemy will attempt an invasion of any part of the coast described, with a view to retain it, and less so for the purpose of desolation. It is nevertheless possible, and being so, provision ought to be made against the danger. An unprotected coast may invite attacks which would not otherwise be thought of. It is believed that the arrangement proposed will be adequate, and that none can be advised, to be so, which would prove more economical."

Monroe's economical defense plan for Chesapeake Bay may have contained in it the elements of America's destiny. For in 1813 it invited British depredations that fanned a patriotic fervor which, in 1814, won for America's militia, soldiers, and seamen their Second War of Independence—and brought the United States her national anthem.

2

MARAUDERS IN CHESAPEAKE BAY: 1813

I

O PINIONS IN ENGLAND differed on how to fight the American war. William Cobbett, an Englishman who had lived in the United States upwards of eight years, published his ideas for staging a sharp offense.

"There will be no difficulty in sending an army of 50,000 to 80,000 men besides sailors and marines," he wrote. "To prevent their landing would be impossible; and it is hardly necessary to say that the whole of the ships of the States, and all the maritime towns, must fall upon the approach of only the fourth part of such an army; unless the Americans should, previous to its landing, be cured of their self-confidence, and lay by the plough for a while for the use of the musket."

Cobbett estimated a year's war in America and wisely pointed out: "The undertaking would be by no means chimerical though, in the *end*, I think it would fail."

Britain's sea lords proposed otherwise. The Admiralty announced 12 August 1812 in the *London Gazette:*

Admiral Sir John Borlase Warren, Bart., K.B., is appointed commander in chief of His Majesty's squadron on the Halifax and West India stations, and down the whole coast of America.

And instead of soldiers, the Admiralty gave Warren instructions to discuss peace with America on the basis of Britain's revoking its Orders in Council.

A senior admiral sent out to negotiate rather than fight, Warren ran into bad-weather delays, lost a sloop of his squadron with all hands in a gale, and reached Halifax after victories at sea had lifted American morale. From President Madison he learned that Britain would have to stop impressing sailors from American ships before the United States would even consider negotiation.

An ingratiating man, with a Cambridge M.S. degree and seventeen years of war behind him, Warren had proved himself a hard-working fleet administrator and, as a flag officer, had picked up considerable diplomatic experience. Nobody's fool, although Admiral Horatio Nelson looked on him as something of a humbug, Warren could promise freedom from hostilities, issue licenses to send trading vessels out on the high seas. He had the power to work out a peace with any portion of the United States that might want to negotiate separately.

Warren also could use his naval might in place of diplomacy. And when, 27 November, the British government first directed him to blockade Delaware and Chesapeake Bays, he eyed those waters as likely locations for carrying out a Cabinet fiat to "chastise the Americans into submission."

Delaware Bay, river-narrow at its head and open to the Atlantic Ocean's sweep at its mouth, offered comparatively small enticement. But Chesapeake Bay held prospects of grandest scope for a marauding fleet.

This beautiful inland sea, 4 to 40 miles wide, stretched 200 miles north from its comparatively narrow mouth between Capes Henry and Charles, named for the sons of King James I. It passed through Virginia and Maryland, fed on both sides by many rivers. From its western mainland shore it absorbed the Elizabeth, James, York, Rappahannock, Potomac, Patuxent, Severn, Patapsco, Susquehanna, and diverse minor tributaries; along its eastern peninsula shore it swallowed the Pocomoke, Nanticoke, Choptank, Chester, Sassafras, Elk, and tributary creeks. A British fleet could sail about anywhere in this bay.

Along the Chesapeake's rivers lay thriving communities whose life and trade depended in large part on bay transportation. As the Atlantic coast provided America's main highway for freight—taking an estimated one-tenth the time and one-hundredth the cost of overland transportation—so the Chesapeake and its rivers carried goods inland to Richmond, Washington, and west; to Baltimore, Havre de Grace, and north. Sloops and market shallops sailed passengers as well as merchandise over the bay. Such rich traffic held out a golden invitation to British marauding.

The bay yielded the finest of foods. Its fishermen took striped bass, bluefish, yellow and white perch, trout, hardheads, flounders, and turtles, netted the sweetest of crabs, and dug the tastiest of oysters. Along the bay's shores, hunters shot squirrels, rabbits, quail. The British could eat well in the Chesapeake.

Up the contiguous rivers abounded lush vegetation—mulberry and hackberry trees, white and pink crepe myrtle, cedars, dark-leaf elms, Chinese silk with blooms of yellow, butternuts, honeysuckle, greenbriar, Virginia creeper, trumpet vines. Here the British could find fresh water. And on the bay's islands, almost entirely sand with few or no trees, "if a small hole is dug in the sand not more than two feet deep it will immediately fill with fresh and pleasant water."

With its lovely plantation countryside, Chesapeake Bay favored Virginia and Maryland with an ideal environment for the American spirit. In these parts, among the farmers' cabins as well as the planters' big houses, had grown much of America's hatred of British domination. And up the Potomac lay

Washington, very home of present American insubordination. The area provided fine targets for chastisement.

Into this bay, 4 February 1813, sailed a British squadron that comprised two ships-of-the-line, three frigates, two sloops, and a forty-one-year-old commander named George Cockburn.

Warren's second-in-command in American waters, London-born Rear-Admiral George Cockburn brought to his new assignment a "rough, overbearing, vain, and capricious" personality. His ruthless temperament had raised this arrogant young man to high command from the bottom of the naval ladder. On H.M.S. *Recourse*'s book as captain's servant at age 9, in service in the East Indies at 14, he had his own ship at 21, and made rear-admiral at 40.

In flagship *Marlborough*, 74 guns, Cockburn arrived eager to lay waste the countryside in water-and-land raids which he and his fellow officers looked upon as frolics.

But the poor calibre of his seamen brought problems, aggravated by living at sea. Kept on board ship for unconscionably long periods, sailors and marines fell victim to many normal shipborne ailments; when set to work or to march on shore after long idleness, with run-down constitutions and flabby muscles, they fell ill to more land-borne diseases.

These "diseases incident to armies" included "coughs, sore throat, pleurisy, peripneumony, rheumatism, intermitting fevers (spring and autumnal), quartan fevers, dropsy, vomiting, cholera morbus, diarrhoea, dysentery, inflammation of the intestines, phrenzy, haemorrhage of the nose, continued fever, scurvy, lues venerea, itch, and worms."

Seamen started deserting shortly after the British fleet set up its blockade and began to chase, capture, and burn market and oyster boats and pleasure craft; to burn barns, bridges, cottages, and stables; and, midnights, to plunder unprotected dwellings. The *Norfolk Herald* of 3 March reported:

> On Friday last five English sailors belonging to the *Dragon* (74 guns), and who had been put as a prize crew

under the command of a midshipman on board a captured vessel, took an opportunity, while the officer was below, to make their escape in a boat and come ashore near Hampton. . . .

On Sunday, four others from the same ship made their escape under similar circumstances . . . they were then furnished with passports and set off to the interior. One of these men had been fourteen years at sea, and during that time had never set foot on land! . . .

Report says that thirty-nine men, who were employed on a watering expedition up James River, made their escape. . . .

But Rear-Admiral Cockburn—ruthless, determined—did not let such defections stop him. From Great Britain's hydrographical office he had excellent charts of Chesapeake Bay, from Britain's Cabinet he had orders to chastise the Americans into submission, and he had the guns and ammunition to fulfill an inborn desire to plunder.

He set about marauding Chesapeake Bay with single-minded purpose.

2

RUMORS OF BLOCKADE reached Chesapeake Bay in the closing days of January. Fishermen reported British warships off the coast, expresses from Princess Anne County in Virginia confirmed Cockburn's approach, and Secretary of the Treasury Albert Gallatin ordered all beacon lights extinguished, including that in the first federal-built lighthouse which had gone up on Cape Henry in 1791.

The United States had two frigates in the Chesapeake: *Constellation*, 36 guns, Captain Charles Stewart, in the Severn at Annapolis; *Adams*, 24 guns, Captain Charles Morris, undergoing renovation in the Potomac at the Washington Navy Yard.

Ready for sea, Capt. Stewart left Annapolis for Hampton Roads 1 February, carried down the bay by a favoring winter breeze. With Yorktown under *Constellation*'s lee 4 February, lookouts sighted Cockburn's squadron heading close-hauled from the Atlantic for the capes.

One of Commodore Edward Preble's lieutenants at Tripoli and a skillful seaman, Capt. Stewart thought fast. He could not run out between the capes past the invading Britishers . . . if he turned back up the bay he must beat to windward as the Britishers now did, and a chase might end badly before he could slip into one of the upper rivers. So he raced Cockburn to Hampton Roads, aiming for haven in the Elizabeth River behind Norfolk.

With flooding tide to help, he kedged his way up the Elizabeth, Cockburn astern. Conditions favored Capt. Stewart in these waters he knew well. When night fell and the tide turned, he found himself in the position he had aimed for, with Cockburn forced to anchor. *Constellation* lay safe, but *Marlborough* and the British squadron had her bottled up.

After setting a small force to keep watch on the American frigate Cockburn could freely range Chesapeake Bay, for only gunboats remained to defend the area.

Sloop- or schooner-rigged for close combat, Navy gunboats went to ninety tons and, like frigates, carried long guns, sometimes carronades, all of smooth bore. Long guns—described by the weight of the round shot they fired—came in iron and brass and ran in 1½-, 2-, 3-, 6-, 9-, 12-, 18-, 24-, 36-, and 42-pound sizes; 1½- and 2-pounders fired on swivels, the larger usually on heavy wood carriages with wheels. An iron 18-pounder, served by nine men, weighed 4,200 pounds, rode a carriage weighing upwards of 800 pounds, and fired more than a mile effectively. A brass 36-pounder weighed 6,860 pounds on a 1,200- to 1,300-pound carriage; manned by fourteen men, it could do damage up to a mile and a half.

Carronades did the close work. A 32-pounder weighed only 1,714 pounds; a 42-pounder needed only four gunners. Named for the Scottish town of Carron which cast the first such cannons, short and wide-muzzled, they threw a heavy shot, with small powder charge, point-blank.

On the coasts of Georgia and the Carolinas, and in Long Island Sound, the big Navy gunboats carried such armament to guard groups of American vessels from depredations by the boats of British frigates. In the Chesapeake, however, gunboats came in smaller sizes and maneuvered largely with sweeps. Fifty to 75 feet long, sometimes lateen-rigged for sail under favorable conditions, they carried upwards of forty men for the great oars and a long 12- or 18-pound gun on a pivot.

Under Jefferson, gunboats had constituted the United States Navy. Denmark had considerable success with them, in quiet water. And Com. Preble's boys—Stephen Decatur, Thomas Macdonough, Richard Somers, *et al*—had towed borrowed Italian gunboats across the Mediterranean to brilliant victories against the Barbary pirates. But in American waters gunboats proved of no utility other than to convoy.

According to Theodore Roosevelt, the main reason for this failure lay in the boats themselves. "They were utterly useless except in perfectly calm weather, for in any wind the heavy guns caused them to career over so as to make it difficult to keep them right side up, and impossible to fire.

"Even in smooth water they could not be fought at anchor, requiring to be kept in position by means of sweeps; and they were very unstable, the recoil of the guns causing them to roll so as to make it difficult to aim with any accuracy after the first discharge, while a single shot hitting one put it *hors de combat*."

This last seldom happened, however, "for they were not often handled with any approach to temerity and, on the contrary, usually made their attacks at a range that rendered it as impossible to inflict as to receive harm.

"It does not seem as if they were very well managed; but they were such ill-conditioned craft that the best officers might be pardoned for feeling uncomfortable in them. Their operations throughout the war offer a painfully ludicrous commentary on Jefferson's remarkable project of having our Navy composed exclusively of such craft."

They had the net effect of giving the Chesapeake's inhabitants unreasonable expectation of security.

Earlier, the *New York Morning Post* had pointed up the bleak situation that existed when Americans entered the War of Independence:

> Without arms, without clothing, without money, and without credit, we took the field; relying upon stout hearts, and the assistance of God, for the success of a righteous cause. The event has proved that, with such reliances, a nation has nothing to fear.

Well . . . with their only two available frigates bottled up and their gunboats affording scant protection, Chesapeake's countryfolk faced Cockburn's squadron with their stout hearts.

For the most part planters and farmers, they also had the muskets, rifles, and pistols with which they brought down local game. But, unlike the frontiersmen who had defeated the British the first time, they had small practical knowledge of how to fight with such arms as the American constitution gave them the right to bear. And when a neighbor shouted that redcoated British marines had landed, they met the invaders in whatever clothes they could snatch as they dashed out of their houses.

This attitude put Cockburn on a perennial spot. Except in the case of some un-uniformed Portuguese militia in Britain's war on the Peninsula, Cockburn had faced only fighters clad in proper military garb. By his code, armed men caught out of uniform became liable to death and their houses, even their towns, liable to the torch.

Too, according to regulations, the invading force respected civilian property; it simply bought what it needed in the way of supplies and paid for what it took. But the situations into which Virginia and Maryland citizens plunged Cockburn proved more complex than that.

For example, he could not expediently detach vessels from his squadron to fetch drinking water from Bermuda or Halifax. Nor could he let his men feed on salt meat when, from the decks of their ships, they could see fat cattle browsing on shore. So he sent to the Chesapeake's farms for fresh water and food.

There the Americans gave him a bad time.

When his landing parties arrived to fill their water casks, the natives shot at his men; with or without water cask, a British redcoat became legitimate game for any fowling-piece owner. When shore parties sought to buy fresh provisions, farmers would not part with cows or even chickens for either silver or gold coin, and they scoffed at British paper money offered for American livestock. It had no value in Maryland or Virginia, they told Cockburn, and no Chesapeake landholder had any desire to go to London to redeem the tender.

Angry and outraged, Cockburn deplored the "useless rancour" of bay citizens.

Many of these citizens came from families that had cultivated land in the Chesapeake Bay country for two hundred years. They had cultivated their minds, also, and their tastes. Cockburn's blockade kept them on short rations of bare necessities, and it seemed to them evidence of renewed determination on Britain's part to acquire a commercial monopoly through her naval power. Exports had begun to fall off. (In Virginia they dropped from $4,800,000 in 1811 to $17,581 in 1814; in Maryland, from $4,500,000 to $238,000.) Importantly, too, the British offered freedom to any Negro slaves who would declare for the invaders.

Squirming under these pressures, a few men took the easy way out. Some made personal deals with landing parties. Others accepted British licenses for their vessels to trade with Spain and Portugal, largely in flour and corn which eventually fed Wellington's army; carrying local newspapers, these vessels also provided much of the intelligence that kept Warren, Cockburn, and the British navy abreast of American offensive and defensive operations on land and sea.

To end such traffic, Navy Secretary William Jones finally sent a general order to commanding officers of United States stations and vessels. Ex-sea captain, ex-Congressman, Philadelphia shipowner William Jones lacked brilliance. But his past showed capability. Since January 1813 in the post he had declined during Jefferson's administration, the Secretary of the Navy wrote, 29 July 1813:

> The palpable and criminal intercourse held with the enemy's forces, blockading and invading the waters and shores of the U. States, is, in a military view, an offence of so deep a die as to call for the vigilant interposition of all the naval officers of the United States.
>
> This intercourse is not only carried on by foreigners, under the specious garb of friendly flags, who convey provisions, water, and succours of all kinds (ostensibly destined for friendly ports, in the face, too, of a declared and rigorous blockade) direct to the fleets and stations of the enemy, with constant intelligence of our naval and military force and preparation, and the means of continuing and conducting the invasion to the greatest possible annoyance of the country; but the same traffic, intercourse, and intelligence is carried on with great subtilty and treachery, by profligate citizens, who, in vessels ostensibly navigating our waters, from port to port, under cover of night, or other circumstances favouring their turpitude, find means to convey succours or intelligence to the enemy, and elude the penalty of the law. This lawless trade and intercourse is also carried on to a great extent in craft whose capacity exempts them from the regulations of the revenue laws, and from the vigilance which vessels of great capacity attract.
>
> I am therefore commanded by the President of the United States to enjoin and direct all naval commanding officers to exercise the strictest vigilance, and to stop or detain all vessels or craft, whatsoever, proceeding, or apparently intending to proceed, towards the enemy's vessels within the waters, or hovering about the harbours, of

the United States; or towards any station occupied by the enemy, within the jurisdiction of the United States, from which vessels or craft the enemy might derive succours or intelligence.

Legitimate traders meanwhile gave the British Chesapeake fleet a gradual warm-up for spring and summer action. On 8 February American letter-of-marque *Lottery*, Bombay-bound from Baltimore, tried to slip past the capes. When Lieutenant Kelly Nazer and 200 men in nine boats attacked *Lottery* in a calm, Captain John Southcomb's twenty-five men and six 12-pounders repelled boarders obstinately. But the American vessel finally lost her captain and nineteen men killed or wounded; the British boats lost thirteen in making the capture.

A month later, 16 March, Lieutenant James Polkingthorne rowed five boats and 105 men into the Rappahannock after privateer schooner *Dolphin*, seventy men and twelve guns, and letters-of-marque *Racer*, *Arab*, and *Lynx*, each carrying thirty men and six guns. The British pulled 15 miles, gallantly dashed at the superior foe, forced *Arab* and *Lynx* into immediate surrender, took *Racer*, turned her guns on *Dolphin* and watched most of that schooner's crew jump overboard. The Americans lost sixteen killed or wounded, the British thirteen.

3

IN MARCH, Warren joined Cockburn with his flagship *San Domingo*, 74 guns, bringing two more ships-of-the-line, three more frigates, and supply vessels. By April, with *Constellation* guarded, the two admirals had the situation at the Chesapeake's mouth well in hand. And to apply Britain's rod of chastisement where it would do most good, Warren ordered Cockburn and the fleet to that "nest of pirates" at the bay's head—Baltimore. En route, he proposed, Cockburn could probe every mark of importance with surfboats carrying six-pounders.

Cockburn's plan for these frolics was—as he broadcast via American visitors to his flagship and released prisoners from lumber, oyster, and other small trading vessels he'd captured —"to land without offering molestation to the unopposing inhabitants, either in their persons or properties; to capture or destroy all articles of merchandise and munitions of war; to be allowed to take off, upon paying the full market price, all such cattle and supplies as the British squadron might require; but, should resistance be offered, or menaces held out, to consider the town as a fortified post and the male inhabitants as soldiers; the one to be destroyed, the other, with their cattle and stock, to be captured."

The invading fleet comprised ships-of-the-line, frigates, brigs, and accompanying tenders which included captured and converted American craft. At different times the flotilla totaled fifteen or more vessels, often broken up into several squadrons.

The fleet started slowly up the bay's western shore, alarming the immediate neighborhood and putting distant countryside into a state of unceasing anxiety, suspenseful waiting. Militia assembled, stood by until exhausted, then went home.

Though Cockburn had announced his intention to cut off war supplies, destroy foundries, and seize public stores by penetrating the rivers at the head of the Chesapeake, his tenders and barges went on frolics into most of the bay's navigable inlets, his marines and sailors plundering and burning with a free hand as they went. At Urbanna on the Rappahannock, he left cannonballs in the brick tobacco warehouse; his men ravaged "Rosegill" mansion, built in 1650 and containing Virginia's second largest library. In the Severn, he brought alarmed citizens of Annapolis out of bed at 3 A.M.

On 16 April Cockburn's advanced squadrons arrived off the Patapsco River where the assembled fleet blockaded the city of Baltimore so effectively that during the week ending 24 April not a single vessel succeeded in getting out of or into Baltimore harbor.

The city had prepared for Cockburn's visit, appropriating $20,000 for defense; citizens had loaned an additional $20,000.

Lookout boats stood at the Patapsco's mouth to signal to cavalry, infantry, and artillery stationed along the river.

Cockburn sent a flag of truce ashore, ostensibly with a letter for Secretary of States James Monroe, but the flag got only to within 4 miles of the city. The officer in charge had seen enough; Cockburn did not attack.

Not so able as Baltimore to defend themselves, smaller towns put up what resistance they could to British vandalism. Sharp's, Tilghman's, and Poplar Islands off the eastern shore, which Cockburn "visited" on his cruise north, also had faced the same problem when the British kept possession for several days and took what supplies they needed: Should the islands' citizens fight, suffer a useless beating, and inevitably lose their stocks, or should they let the invaders take freely and hope the national government would indemnify them?

Now Poole's Island, some 25 miles above Baltimore, and Spesutie Island, less than 10 miles below Havre de Grace, had the British fleet descend on them and for two weeks make off with their cattle and their hogs. The islands' inhabitants thoroughly incensed, Maryland's Governor Levin Winder wrote President Madison 26 April that the common defense lay with the national government "and to us it is a most painful reflection that after every effort we have made, or can make, for the security of our citizens and their property, they have little to rely on but the possible forbearance of the enemy."

Already proved a weak reed for American householders to rely on, British forbearance held up for a few days only before it wilted completely. During that time, Warren sent Cockburn farther up the bay with a light squadron of two frigates and a half dozen attendant vessels; they carried about 400 marines and seamen, in nearly equal numbers, constituting a naval brigade, with a half dozen army artillerists.

Cockburn went into the Elk River (where George Washington had taken shipping on his way to the siege of Yorktown thirty years before). On 29 April Cockburn sent Lieutenant George A. Westphal of *Marlborough* with thirteen barges to attack Frenchtown, a relay point for Baltimore–Philadelphia stages.

Against four 4-pounders which since the Revolution had seen service only as ballast in a fishing vessel, Lieut. Westphal did not lose a single man. He routed stage drivers and wagoners who, with a few militiamen from Elkton, manned the town's redoubt. He then plundered Frenchtown's wharf and fishery, and from the warehouses took army clothing, saddles, bridles, and other cavalry equipment valued at upwards of $30,000. After which he fired the warehouses, along with a Susquehanna River packet-boat and four small craft. Lieut. Westphal's men did not ransack or burn any homes.

From Spesutie Island, his base of operations, Cockburn had kept the citizens of Havre de Grace on tenterhooks since 20 April when word of his nearby presence first reached them. Living quietly on the Susquehanna's west bank about 2 miles above the bay, where a bar obstructed navigation, these townsfolk had a considerable herring fishery trade and about sixty homes.

They made immediate defensive preparations, calling in several militia companies with little discipline and no arms. Then, from the governor had come some arms, and volunteers had mounted one 9-pounder and two 6-pounders in the "Potato Battery" breastwork on a high bank just below town and placed one 18-pounder and two 9-pounders on Concord Point where river and bay joined. They had hoisted an American flag over the Point battery and set patrols to stand watch every night.

Overcome by continued excitement and incessant manual labor, however, and seeing that Cockburn's squadron—which arrived off the town 28 April—continued to frolic on outlying islands and opposite shore towns, a large part of Havre de Grace's defenders went home.

On Saturday afternoon, 1 May, a British deserter brought word to Havre de Grace that Cockburn had scheduled an attack for Sunday night, and the town prepared again.

Women and children fled into back country. Sunday night 250 militia stood to arms, horsemen patrolled, and Concord Point's battery volunteers manned their cannons. But Cockburn did not show, and exhausted townsfolk, believing themselves hoaxed, fell back into bed.

Having learned about his deserter, Cockburn had only put off action to lull Havre de Grace into false security; at daybreak on Monday, 3 May, some fifteen to twenty British barges pulled for shore.

When Concord Point's battery opened on them, the raiders returned the fire with Congreve rockets and, rounding the point, landed and panicked the town. They scattered women and children into neighboring woods. They confused the militiamen, conferring on a soldier named Webster the doubtful honor of being the first, perhaps the only, American killed by a rocket in the War of 1812. They took the "Potato Battery" and captured John O'Neil who, practically singlehanded, had tried to hold them off. With the town beginning to flame, they turned Concord Point's guns as well as their own on Havre de Grace.

Sunrise saw the British march into the town's central square. Separated here into bands of thirty or forty, marines and seamen received orders to plunder and burn every house not already on fire. While one division of fifty men marched nearly a mile into the country, pursuing the militia, the others stayed in town and had an extraordinary frolic.

Each man with a hatchet in his belt, they went into houses by groups, hacked open wardrobes and bureaus, seized what articles they liked, fired the homes, and moved on. Cannonfire ceased, but the crackle of flames and the crash of falling house timbers filled Havre de Grace.

Two or three women refused to leave their houses, and when Cockburn stepped ashore to watch his men's malicious burning the women succeeded in persuading him to spare their homes. By then upwards of forty of the town's sixty dwellings had gone up in flames, and those that still stood bore scars of cannon and musket balls.

Two British barges went 5 miles upriver to the head of navigation where they expected to find many local vessels. But, scuttled, these lay on the river bottom, later to be raised without essential damage. The party burned a warehouse on shore.

Sated with their frolic after four hours, the main invasion body put Concord Point's guns into their surfboats and went back to their ships, while Cockburn pushed 8 miles north of Havre de Grace with a small detachment to destroy Colonel Samuel Hughes's furnace which made public cannons. The admiral also destroyed twenty-eight 32-pounders ready for sending away, eight other long guns, and four carronades in the boring house and foundry, and five 24-pounders in a battery protecting the furnace.

By sunset his barges passed down the bay, rejoined the squadron, and he reported to Bermuda-bound Warren:

"Our small division has been during the whole of this day on shore, in the centre of the enemy's country, and on his high road between Baltimore and Philadelphia."

Proud of these accomplishments, Cockburn apparently cared little that they raised national indignation as vivid first-hand newspaper reports spread over the United States:

The conduct of the sailors while on shore was exceedingly rude and wanton. The officers gave such of the inhabitants as remained behind liberty to carry out such articles of furniture as they chose while the sailors were plundering their houses; but the sailors, not content with pillaging and burning, broke and defaced these also as they were standing in the streets. Elegant looking-glasses were dashed in pieces, and beds were ripped open for the sport of scattering the feathers in the wind. These outrages to be sure, were not commanded by the officers, but they were not restrained by them.

Little can be said, indeed, in favor of the officers' conduct in this particular. They selected tables and bureaus for their private use, and after writing their names on them, sent them on board the barges. The Admiral himself was pleased with an elegant coach which fell in his way, and commanded it to be put on board a boat, which belonged to the proprietor of the ferry, and taken to his ship. This order was executed, although he was told it belonged to a poor coach-maker whose family must suffer by its loss.

But the most distressing part of the scene was at the close of the day, when those who fled in the morning returned to witness the desolation of their homes, and the ruin of all their possessions.

When citizens of Havre de Grace went to Cockburn under a flag of truce, he refused to return any private property. Instead, he callously told them he could not commend their courage in suffering 500 men to land and plunder their town. Two days after burning Havre de Grace, 5 May, Cockburn went up the quiet Sassafras River on the bay's eastern shore with Lieut. Westphal. They took 150 men and five guns. On the way to the villages of Georgetown and Fredericktown, almost facing each other on opposite sides of the river, the landing party captured two American lookouts in a small boat.

Cockburn sent the prisoners ahead with his promise not to molest the townsfolk if they stood quietly by while he seized whatever vessels and public property he found and paid for whatever provisions and other items his squadron needed. The skeptical Americans recognized British standard marauding procedure, but went to report the offer.

Having allowed the pair time to deliver his greetings, Cockburn moved upriver to where projecting points of land, about a mile from the two villages, compelled the British boats to proceed in close order. Here, some 300 to 400 American militiamen who did not trust Cockburn's promises opened fire with muskets and a single fieldpiece, wounding five British. After which Cockburn gave Georgetown and Fredericktown the treatment proper for daring to defend themselves, despite the fact that, after their first volley, the militiamen had taken to the woods.

"The British," reported Catherine Knight, 38, a Georgetown eyewitness, "commenced to burn all the lower part of the town, which was largely of frame. There were, however, two brick buildings on top of the hill which had not as yet been fired. In one of them was an old lady sick and almost destitute, and to this building the Admiral and his sailors and marines proceeded at a rapid gait.

"I followed them, but before I got to the top of the hill they had set fire to the house in which the old lady lay. I immediately called the attention of the Admiral to the fact that they were about to burn up a human being, and that a woman, and I pleaded with him to make his men put the fire out.

"This I finally succeeded in doing, when they immediately went next door, not forty feet distant, and fired the second of the brick houses. I told the commanding officer that as the wind was blowing toward the other house the old lady would be burned anyhow, when, apparently affected by my appeal, he called his men off but left the fire burning, saying 'Come on, boys!' As they went out the door, one of them struck his boarding-axe through a panel of the door."

Catherine Knight put the fire out with her broom.

Returning downriver, Cockburn visited a village (Still Pond?) on a branch of the Sassafras. Warned by what had happened above, the folk here shook hands with the admiral and sold him all he asked for.

Deciding that the upper bay region would offer no further armed opposition since he had seen to it that there were "now neither public property, vessels, nor warlike stores remaining in the neighborhood," Cockburn two days later, 7 May, left the area to lick its wounds and sailed down to the capes.

4

WITH WARREN in Bermuda, Cockburn held Chesapeake Bay with one ship-of-the-line and four frigates.

To some extent, American gunboats, under Captain Charles Gordon's alert command, restricted the movements of enemy foraging parties beyond the near range of the British ships. Constantly vigilant, the gunboats hit and ran during calms and favorable local conditions.

Constellation's Capt. Stewart reported to Navy Secretary Jones that the British ". . . act cautiously, and never separate so far from one another that they cannot in the course of a few hours give to each other support, by dropping down or running up, as the wind or tide serve. . . . They do not appear disposed to put anything to risk, or to make an attack where they are likely to meet with opposition."

Manpower problems, seemingly, continued to plague Cockburn. Deserting seamen still went over the sides of British ships in large numbers.

"Their loss in prisoners and deserters has been very considerable," Capt. Stewart reported. "The latter are coming up to Norfolk almost daily, and their naked bodies are frequently fished up on the Bay shore, where they must have been drowned in attempting to swim. They all give the same account of the dissatisfaction of their crews, and their detestation of the service they are engaged in."

Early in June, Warren sailed up from Bermuda with 2,650 reinforcements—1,800 marines, 300 marine artillery, 300 land troops of the Hundred and Second Regiment, and 250 Chasseurs Britannique.

Heading the troops came Major-General Sidney Beckwith with Lieutenant-Colonel Charles James Napier, second in army command. Gen. Beckwith had "the heart and hand for his business"; he wanted to play his full part in chastising the Americans. But Warren and Cockburn wanted the whip applied in their way. As a result, Gen. Beckwith became "sulky when required to do what he deemed silly." Which, in Col. Napier's opinion, made things more silly. As a man, said Col. Napier of Gen. Beckwith, "he certainly is a clever fellow—but a very odd fish."

Though Col. Napier expressed a liking for his commanding general, he disliked serving under him "in his Chesapeake fashion." In fact, Col. Napier looked with a disapproving eye upon the over-all British policy in the bay.

He hoped to keep a tight rein on the unsavory Chasseurs Britannique whom he commanded. These Frenchmen, enlisted from Britain's war prisoners and recently returned from Botany Bay where they had served a period as a punishment, "are duberous [dubious]," he reported. He added:

"Much I dislike sacking and burning of towns; it is bad employment for British troops. This authorized, perhaps needful plundering—though to think so is difficult—is very disgusting. . . . I will with my own hand kill any perpetrator of brutality under my command."

The British assembled, in Lynnhaven Roads, what constituted for the time a first-class amphibious force. They had the know-how and the manpower to tow and kedge their ships and frigates up the bay and into its rivers. With lower gun-decks cleared, some ships-of-the-line carried veteran soldiers trained to take up where marines left off after landing in surfboats and barges. And their sailors could handle mobile guns on land as well as service heavy cannons on board ship, acting in turn as naval gunners and army artillerists.

The main military problem, as Col. Napier saw it, lay in the three-man council of Warren, Cockburn, and Gen. Beckwith; a single head could better guide.

The Admiralty had specifically instructed: ". . . any attempt which should have the effect of crippling the [American] naval force should have a preference."

The trio chose to attack Norfolk. This Elizabeth River area held *Constellation* and large and valuable stores of public property in the Gosport Navy Yard commanded by Captain John Cassin.

To stage a successful sea-land attack, Warren and Gen. Beckwith needed answers to basic questions concerning military defenses around Norfolk. They wrote their questions down, and Cockburn answered them:

"The statement of the number of troops stationed on the

various points around for the defence of Norfolk varies in proportion to the number of people from whom I have endeavored to collect information thereon. But on the whole I am led to conclude there may be about 5,000 men amongst which there are no Regulars whatever, those nearest approaching to such being people of the neighbourhood raised into two regiments under the denomination of 1st and 2nd Volunteers to be stationed at Norfolk for its protection.

"Some time ago the enemy were much stronger in this neighbourhood but since the reduction of our Naval Force in this bay, Major-General Hampden [Wade Hampton], who then commanded here, with several other officers and all the regulars, particularly the Kentucky Regiment (which is stated as a remarkable fine one) have been sent to Canada, and the command again left to General Taylor [Brigadier-General Robert B. Taylor] who I believe never saw a shot fired, and his second in command is a captain of one of the volunteer companies.

"The number there of the enemy and the strength of the ground for bush fighting (it being much covered and not known by us) constitute the only point from which opposition is to be looked for."

Cockburn pointed out that the approach to Craney Island, at the entrance to the Elizabeth River, being shallow and difficult, the island should be previously attacked.

Anchored in the middle of the channel above the island, bottled-up frigate *Constellation* had closed her lower ports and taken every hanging line off her sides. Her boarding nets, boiled in half-made pitch until hard as wire and weighted with pig-iron ballast, hung triced up outboard toward the yard-arms—ready to fall on attacking boats at a hatchet's hack through the tricing lines. Her gunners also had loaded their carronades to the muzzle with musket balls and depressed the guns to sweep the waters close to the ship.

Skirmishes preceded the British attack. On the night of 12 June, Lieutenant John Creerie took fifty men in boats from frigate *Narcissus*, 32, and fell on the small cutter *Surveyor* in York River. *Surveyor*'s six 12-pound carronades out of commission, her captain, William S. Travis, disputed her deck inch by inch with fifteen men and pistols. He lost the cutter, with five wounded; Lieut. Creerie took her with three killed, seven wounded, and admiration for American sea fighters.

On 20 June, fifteen American gunboats under Captain Joseph Tarbell went after becalmed frigate *Junon*, 38, in a typical gunboat action—anchoring at very long range, promptly swinging into a position from which guns could not shoot, getting under way again to close on the feebly defended frigate as a slight breeze sprang up. Whereupon the gunboats becoming almost useless and two other British craft approaching to take a hand, the Americans withdrew.

At daylight 22 June, Warren, Cockburn, and Gen. Beckwith threw their combined forces against Norfolk. To take that town they had first to reduce American positions on the Elizabeth River's channel which, 300 yards from edge to edge, ran through extensive flats.

The first of the American fortifications commanded Craney Island. This flat 35-acre island, part of it always in danger of submersion at high tide, boasted no natural defense. But it now had a well-built system of intrenchments, a battery of four 6-pounders, one 18-pounder, two 24-pounders, and 580 regular Army and militia under Lieutenant-Colonel Henry Beatty—supported by 100 of *Constellation*'s seamen under Lieutenants B. J. Neale, W. B. Shubrick, and James Saunders and fifty marines under Lieutenant Henry B. Breckenridge. The frigate lay near by, and twenty gunboats.

Instead of shelling Craney Island from a distance, the British tried to take it by storm—which posed a very neat problem because of the shoals.

Outward to Hampton Roads for a half mile, these shoals lay under less than 4 feet of water. At low tide, the sand immediately surrounding the island came bare so that infantry could march over from the mainland and flank the island; at high tide, landing parties could row reasonably close and wade ashore in a frontal attack. But how to attack in concert?

The British picked an ebbing tide to land seamen, marines, and soldiers totaling 800 by their count and 2,500 by American estimates. They debarked at Hoffleur Creek in the Nansemond River 4 miles northwest of Craney Island on the mainland. But this flanking move came up against the notoriously good marksmanship of American ships' gunners—and the flankers retreated.

Warren reported to the Admiralty: "In consequence of the representation of the officer commanding the troops of the difficulty of their passing over from the land, I considered that the persevering in the attempt would cost more men than the number with us would permit, as the other forts must have been stormed before the frigate and the dockyard could be destroyed."

The "other forts" included feeble Fort Norfolk on the Elizabeth River's right bank, Fort Nelson on the left, and two small redoubts called Forts Tar and Barbour protecting land approaches to Norfolk.

At 11 A.M., Captain Samuel G. Pechell, commanding the British frontal attack on Craney Island, brought fifteen landing barges and crews, with 500 soldiers, off the island's northwest point. Led by Captain J. M. Hanchett (reputed natural son of King George III), the barges ran into the American battery's barrage of round-, grape-, and canister shot. They ran first into the heavy iron cannon balls . . . then the clusters of a dozen 2-inch balls . . . finally the scattering balls, each as large as two or three musket balls.

Fresh from repelling the British flankers, Craney Island's gunners poured metal into the advancing boats until Capt. Hanchett's 24-oared launch *Centipede* and one or two others grounded and gunfire sank two more in the shallows. As Capt. Cassin wrote Secretary Jones, "the officers of the *Constellation* fired their 18-pounders more like riflemen than artillerists. I never saw such shooting, and seriously believe they saved the island."

Midshipman Josiah Tatnall and crewmen of *Constellation* waded out to the disabled boats, took possession, and brought ashore those of the British party who had thrown away their arms. Capturing green-painted *Centipede*, Midshipman Tatnall found a small terrier dog sitting on the brass 3-pounder "grass-hopper" in the launch's bow. And the invading flotilla—having lost three killed, sixteen wounded, sixty-two missing—made off in disorder.

Thus a total of not less than 1,500 invaders never came to grips with Craney Island's 730 defenders because, as the British claimed, muddy bottom prevented their wading ashore. But the bottom had not stopped Americans from wading out to the boats, and Capt. Cassin reported:

"We have had all day deserters from the army coming in. I have myself taken in twenty-five, and eighteen prisoners belonging to the *Centipede*."

Craney Island's successful defense cost the Americans not a single man killed or wounded.

5

WITHIN THE WEEK, early on 25 June, in retaliation for the humiliating repulse at Craney Island, Gen. Beckwith put 2,000 men under Col. Napier ashore at Hampton, a village across the roads from Norfolk. Cockburn covered the attack with launches and rocket ships.

Hampton's garrison of Major Stapelton Crutchfield and 438 men with four 12-pounders and three 6-pounders lost seven killed before retiring after two assaults; they brought down 210 invaders according to many British officers—48 according to Warren.

Then followed the most wanton mischief Chesapeake Bay had seen. For two days the British pillaged Hampton without restraint. Soldiers and sailors ran wild, chasseurs berserk. They maliciously destroyed private property and public medical stores . . . they grossly abused unarmed men . . . they violated women.

Official American protest of these excesses brought Gen. Beckwith's excuse that, at Craney Island, Americans had fired on British soldiers clinging to a wrecked barge.

"With a feeling natural to such an occasion," Gen. Beckwith told Gen. Taylor, "the troops of that corps landed at Hampton."

To which Gen. Taylor returned a précis of acts which showed that American gunners at Craney had stopped using grape and taken to round shot in order to fire, safely, over the heads of the wrecked sailors at other British boats which continued the attack.

"The troops on the island exerted themselves in acts of kindness to the unresisting foe," Gen. Taylor pointed out.

Gen. Beckwith had nothing more to say. But a few days later he notified Halifax headquarters that he planned to send the chasseurs away. And Col. Napier, looking on the Hampton raid with comparative objectivity, summed up:

"He ought to have hanged several villains at little Hampton . . . every horror was committed with impunity—rape, murder, pillage; and not a man punished!"

Col. Napier recorded the mixed reactions of British soldiers on the scene:

"Well! whatever horrible acts were done at Hampton, they were not done by the Hundred and Second, for they were never let to quit their ranks, and they almost mutinied at my preventing them joining in the sack of the unfortunate town. The marine artillery behaved like soldiers; they had it in their power to join in the sack and refused."

Of the chasseurs—"the greatest rascals existing"—he wrote:

"Much I wished to shoot some, but had no opportunity. They really murdered without any object but the pleasure of murdering."

Though British plundering of the Chesapeake to date had destroyed some property of military value, the frolics that gratified sailors and soldiers too long cooped up on board ship began to cost Britain heavily. For Mr. Madison's War, which had started without unified popular support for an apparently senseless American aggression against friendly Canada, now became a bloody resistance against a barbarous and hateful foreign foe in the Chesapeake. Formerly reluctant citizens now roused themselves to protect their firesides.

As the fleet continued to occupy the bay, British officers found the onus heavy. Noted Col. Napier: "Strong is my dislike to what is perhaps a necessary part of our job, viz., plundering and ruining the peasantry. We drive all their cattle and of course ruin them; my hands are clean, but it is hateful to see the poor Yankees robbed, and to be the robber."

The British fleet went on terrorizing the bay for the rest of the summer, with officers and men improving their knowledge of local sailing and landing conditions.

Warren ordered thirteen vessels 10 miles up the James River and sent the area's inhabitants, remembering Hampton's sack, fleeing from their homes. Lighter craft sailed closer to Richmond, but turned back. And having promised, via the captain of a vessel from Alexandria stopped by the blockade, to teach Mr. Madison the difference between a paper blockade and a blockade of wood and iron, Warren entered the Potomac River 13 July as if to deliver the lesson in person.

His flotilla took soundings and marked a channel with buoys.

Next day they captured American gunboat *Asp*, killed or wounded ten of her crew, and went some 30 miles upriver. From Blakiston Island, Cockburn took frigates and smaller vessels 10 miles farther, to throw a scare into Washington where President Madison lay ill.

Elbridge Gerry, Jr., son of the Vice President, pictured Washington's reaction:

"Alarm guns were fired, and the bells set in motion, and

very soon every person in the city was moving. Soldiers in every direction were mustering, and in a few hours 2 or 3,000 troops were on the march to the fort [Washington, formerly Warburton] 14 miles distant. They were followed by carts loaded with ammunition, provisions, and baggage of all kinds.

"In the afternoon a list was circulated for volunteers, on which list I placed my name. We are for a police guard and a corps to defend the city. Every preparation is making to defend the place, and even now (Saturday) troops are passing in all directions" . . . full, another observer reported, of ardor and enthusiasm.

Despite the alarm, the public did not believe the British ships could get past Kettle Bottom shoals in the Potomac, and Cockburn did not. Two of his vessels grounding, he returned downriver to rejoin the squadron and raid elsewhere. *Niles' Weekly Register* reported:

> They plundered anything and everything, robbing even the women and children of their clothes, and destroying such articles as did not suit them to carry away.

Compelled in self-defense to take up arms, farmers and planters along the Potomac and Patuxent shores neglected crops while they performed military duty, slaves ran off, a poverty-stricken populace fell sick. Some found the burdens of war so difficult to bear that they abandoned their homes and moved to new settlements in the west.

Leaving the Potomac 30 July, the British fleet sailed toward Annapolis and landed on Kent Island in an apparent effort to combat shipboard sicknesses which had killed seventy-four men while in the Potomac. On 8 August the squadron feinted at Baltimore.

Baltimore again sprang to arms, manning its batteries. But Cockburn once more decided against an attack. And from Kent Island Warren and he let citizens of the upper bay know that unless, by the following spring, they elected to state and national office men who favored making peace with England, the British fleet would return in 1814 to destroy Baltimore and desolate both shores of the bay.

Leaving, they attacked Queenstown on the Chester River and, on 10 August at 3 A.M., tried to take St. Michaels, south of Kent Island, where some 500 Easton Fencibles, Mechanic Volunteers, Hearts of Oak, and Independent Volunteers in handsome uniforms waited under Brigadier-General Perry Benson's fine silk flag which the women of the village had worked for him. Eleven British barges, each with a 6-pounder fieldpiece, aimed to destroy the village shipyards and six vessels on the ways.

But the ingenious Marylanders hung lanterns in treetops to misdirect British gunfire. Captain William Dodson, local tradition holds, left by his handsomely dressed companions to defend a shore breastwork with one white man and one Negro, wadded a 27-pound bundle of old scrap iron into the single gun that could train on the invaders. Its blast killed nineteen and it leaped over the parapet to send wading redcoats flying back to their barges.

A deserter reported that Cockburn's nephew, on the eve of going back to England, had begged for "one last frolic against the Yankees." Captain Dodson's gun killed this lieutenant of marines, and Cockburn reportedly said: "He was worth more than the whole damned town!"

British incursions fell off, although some 2,100 sailors and soldiers went on shore for exercise 26 August at Bayside in a "number of small boats so great it was like chips thrown on the water from a basket." And in early November they embarked 170 Negro slaves on captured schooners and took them, with a large part of the blockading fleet, to Bermuda.

For England, Warren and Cockburn's Chesapeake blockade of 1813 had impoverished a large part of the countryside, kept citizens terrorized, immobilized two frigates, and destroyed a modicum of public property. For America, their exploits had made the war more popular and induced both political parties to make greater sacrifices for its support.

Cockburn, the active member of the pair, also had made an impressive start in sending his name down America's generations as the greatest villain of them all.

On the bay itself, an Annapolis banqueter toasted the two admirals:

"May the eternal vengeance of Heaven hurl them to some station that will terminate their inhuman butcheries and savage cruelties. . . ."

Miles from the scene, the *Boston Gazette* declared of Cockburn:

> . . . there breathes not in any quarter of the globe a more savage monster than this same British admiral. He is a disgrace to England and to human nature. . . .

3

INVASION: 1814

IN TWO YEARS of war the United States had done more damage on the seas, Great Britain on land. Together they had lost about 6,000 killed, 12,000 wounded, 6,000 imprisoned. On both sides of the Canadian border some 400 homes had gone up in flames. Public emotion seethed in America and in England, and peace negotiations via Russia bogged down.

With Napoleon's time running out in Europe, Great Britain in 1814 took a fresh look at the campaign against the United States. Large armies and fleets soon could cross the Atlantic to administer proper chastisement. And since Warren had complained of overly onerous duties on the western Atlantic station, a more vigorous admiral could go there to rebuild Britain naval prestige which American frigates and privateers continued to belittle.

Though a strong body of British opinion wanted peace on any honorable terms, the government decided to please those who clamored for an overwhelming conquest of the United States.

Feeling in the United States ran high, too. Josiah Quincy of Massachusetts had told Congress that invasion of Canada was "a wanton and wicked act by which we visited with fire and sword our innocent and unoffending neighbor for the offenses of a nation 3,000 miles distant." Before crossing into their territory, Brigadier-General William Hull in 1812 had warned Canadians that "if you should take part in the approaching contest . . . the horrors and calamities of war will stalk before you."

Both American and British armies had applied the torch to settlements along the border. In newspapers on each side of the Atlantic appeared names like Newark, York, Niagara, River Raisin. Who had started outrages there? Who had retaliated? Who had done what to whom? When had American militiamen and Lake seamen got out of hand? When had British troops and allied Indians ravaged under authority of their officers? Indignation, excuses, counterclaims flew back and forth over the ocean.

American feeling attributed British atrocities to animosities aroused in the Revolution, to Britain's jealousy of her former colony's rapid commercial rise, and to plain outrage over the way Yankee ships and sailors made free of the high seas which Britain claimed to rule.

Two of the Canadian incidents had ultimate effect on British actions in the Chesapeake during the summer of 1814.

One of these took place at the first seat of Upper Canada's legislature—Newark. America's Secretary of War John Armstrong had given permission to destroy the town on the understanding that American defense of Fort George—on the Canadian side of the Niagara River—"may render it proper." Abandoning the border fort, Brigadier-General George McClure gave the town twelve hours' notice at dusk on 10 December 1813 (he later declared) and invited its citizens—as the War Secretary had suggested in case of defense need—"to remove themselves and their effects to some place of greater safety."

Britain claimed that the attractive little settlement of 150 houses, with snow on the ground, had 149 of its dwellings in flames in far less than twelve hours and saw "some 400 women and children turned out of doors to face the winter night."

The second incident involved Upper Canada's capital city of York (now Toronto). According to British visitor, John M. Duncan, the place contained little more than a single small street "and the Parliament house is discovered to have been only a wooden one." Dr. John Strachen, later first Bishop of Toronto, described the Parliament house as brick-walled, consisting of "two elegant halls, with convenient offices for the accommodation of the Legislature and the Courts of Justice."

After Brigadier-General Zebulon Pike led a victorious American assault against York 27 April 1813 and died in a random powder magazine explosion, his men found themselves on the town. For three days the soldiers, along with seamen of Captain Isaac Chauncey's Lake Ontario fleet, had flare-ups with the Canadians. On 30 April the Parliament house burst into flames.

Through the smoke of years, a few facts stand out: a party of ransacking American sailors, without officers, found a human scalp hanging in Parliament behind the Speaker's chair, with his mace. Envisaging the scalp as an official Canadian government trophy, the outraged sailors threw the capitol library's books and government records into piles and set them on fire. They sent the scalp to Capt. Chauncey who passed it on to Major-General Henry Dearborn; the mace went to Washington, where it stayed 120 years.*

Canada's governor-general, George Prevost, who had offered to conduct the war more humanely if the Americans did likewise, proclaimed that "prompt and signal vengeance will be taken for every fresh departure by the enemy from that system of warfare which ought alone to subsist between enlightened and civilized nations."

In London, plans took shape to send troops down Lake Champlain from Montreal to New York, to blockade the entire American coast while making diversionary strikes from

* See Notes, Chap. III.

Maine to the Carolinas, and to invade the United States through the Gulf of Mexico. Concerted activities shaped up in June of 1814.

To command the fleet assembling in Bermuda for stepped-up Chesapeake Bay operations, the British Admiralty sent fifty-six-year-old Vice-Admiral Alexander Forrester Inglis Cochrane. A most successful exponent of amphibious warfare, Alexander Cochrane had put an army ashore in Egypt in 1801; in 1809 he had reduced Martinique with a combined land-and-sea attack.

Considered a younger man among British admirals, he carried himself with authority; a large nose dominated his thin-cheeked face. Critics mentioned his cupidity, his harsh treatment of faithful bluejackets, his callous willingness to sacrifice troops. His friends called him active, able, original . . . and lucky.

Together with his proven ability and his reputation for luck, Admiral Alexander Cochrane brought over the ocean with him an ingrained resentment of America. For, after his cousin, the seventh Earl of Dundonald, had died fighting with Americans against the French at the siege of Louisburg, other ungrateful Americans had killed his brother Charles at Yorktown in 1781.

Some of Cochrane's assembling ships, under Rear-Admiral Poulteney Malcolm, carried troops from Wellington's army— a large detachment from the south of Spain and soldiers previously employed in the siege of Bayonne and embarked at Bordeaux without any leave to go home.

To help him "destroy and lay waste such towns and districts upon the coasts" as they might find assailable, and to convert the Chesapeake into a British lake when he arrived from Bermuda, Cochrane had for second-in-command—Cockburn. Cockburn returned to the bay in March.

Meanwhile, Captain Robert Barrie in *Dragon*, 74, had kept a winter watch on the bay. Frigate *Adams* had slipped out to sea in January. *Constellation*, however, trying twice in February, could not escape. Now, to resist Cochrane's forthcoming drive in the Chesapeake, Navy Secretary Jones called on fabulous Joshua Barney, a legend even in his own times.

Born on a farm near Baltimore, one of fourteen children, Barney had worked the bay and the ocean off Cape Henry in a pilot boat at the age of eleven. Passing twelve in January of 1771, he sailed to Liverpool in his brother-in-law's gale-battered brig and in two years became a second mate. In the middle of the Atlantic in 1775 Joshua Barney found himself in command of a leaking ship whose captain died en route to the Mediterranean. Not only did the youngster reach Nice, but he insisted on payment for the vessel's cargo, found himself thrown into prison by the governor, escaped, appealed to the British minister at Milan, returned to Nice, received an apology from the governor, took his pay, and went home—his job properly done.

On returning to the Chesapeake and learning that the Revolution had started, he volunteered in small vessels. As lieutenant he later went on board U. S. brig *Andrew Doria*, 14 guns, saw America's new 13-stripe flag given its first official salute at St. Eustatius in Dutch West Indies 16 November 1776, took a British prize back to Cape Henry through December gales, and ended up a prisoner of war on ship *Perseus*.

Exchanged for an English lieutenant, he joined U. S. frigate *Virginia*, 28 guns, in the bay, captured a British barge while out reconnoitering in a pilot boat, and when *Virginia* unhappily tried to get to sea three months later, again found himself a prisoner on board British frigate *Emerald*. Exchanged a second time, he took command of a privateer schooner carrying two guns and eight men, met up with a larger British privateer of four guns and sixty men whose captain, disliking the bother of prisoners, put him ashore.

His three captures established Joshua Barney, at nineteen, in the British fleet as a good enemy and, because he gave humane treatment to prisoners he himself had taken, he received good treatment.

In 1780, at sea in U. S. sloop-of-war *Saratoga*, 20 guns, he started home in command of a prize, and a day later fell into British hands. This time the enemy sent him to England, put him in Mill Prison, and set a price on his head when he escaped after three months. He lived unrecognized in London for six weeks, slipped over to the Continent, and found his way back to Philadelphia by spring of 1782, still full of fight.

The state of Pennsylvania gave him command of converted merchantman *Hyder Ally*, 16 guns and 110 men, to convoy a fleet of trading vessels down Delaware Bay. Chased by a British frigate and a sloop-of-war, he enticed the sloop into capture and returned with the convoy to Philadelphia, bringing 18-gun *General Monk* as a brilliant trophy of the Revolution's last important naval action.

Joshua Barney then sailed *General Monk* to France, where Marie Antoinette bestowed on him a public kiss that brought others from the ladies of the court and created a song, "Barney, Leave the Girls Alone." When Britain, and Benjamin Franklin, signed the Revolution's peace treaty, Barney brought home first news that King George had recognized American independence.

After Congress in 1794 ordered six frigates laid down, the U. S. Navy listed Joshua Barney as number-four captain, behind John Barry, Samuel Nicholson, and Silas Talbot. Feeling unjustly rated behind Talbot—new to the Navy—Barney declined to serve. Instead, he went with the French until 1802, as captain and commodore. As commander-in-chief, he participated in the Santo Domingo expedition.

But, proponent of a strong American Navy, he offered his services in 1807 to Jefferson and in 1809 to Madison, neither of whom found a place for him. When, therefore, hostilities with Great Britain opened in 1812, Joshua Barney wasted no time with government bureaus. Leaving his farm and his young and beautiful second wife in Anne Arundel County, this past-fifty patriot took command of Baltimore privateer schooner *Rossie* with ten 12-pounders and 120 men.

On his single voyage in *Rossie*, 12 July to 10 November 1812, he captured four ships, eight brigs, three schooners, and three sloops whose value, with cargoes, totaled more than $1,500,000.

When the Navy Secretary offered him command of a gunboat flotilla fitting out in Baltimore for the Chesapeake, he accepted with one condition—that he receive his orders exclusively from the Navy Department. With nearly forty years of experience behind him, he wanted no hamstringing by youngsters.

Com. Barney had the fleet of twenty-six gunboats fitted out by April of 1814 and accepted his appointment as a captain 27 April, his command comprising 900 men officered by shipmasters and mates, mostly volunteers, enrolled in Baltimore.

At the end of May Com. Barney took sixteen vessels down the bay to attack Tangier Island, off the Potomac River, where Cockburn had established an encampment. Here, British warships could bring their prizes, ride in safety, and obtain fresh water. Here, British troops could store arms and ammunition and find refreshment between battles.

On 1 June, a little below the Patuxent, on his flagship—sloop *Scorpion*, 8 carronades and a long gun, with son Major William Bedford Barney of the Marine Corps acting as his aide—Com. Barney chased British schooner *St. Lawrence*, 13, and seven other enemy vessels in a lively action until *Dragon*'s seventy-four heavy guns forced him into the Patuxent. British reinforcements coming up to blockade his gunboats, the commodore took them into the shallow waters of St. Leonard's Creek.

To ferret the American flotilla out, Cockburn on 8 June sent 800 men in twenty-one barges, a rocket ship, and two schooners mounting 32-pounders. Barney moved downstream to meet them with 500 men in thirteen boats, his flagship a barge with crew of 20.

The fleets pelted each other with grapeshot and musket balls. One of Britisher William Congreve's case-rockets—which could travel 3,000 yards with uncertain aim—exploded like shrapnel in the open hatch of an American barge. Passing through a seaman, it set the boat on fire, and ignited a barrel of gunpowder. Asking permission to board the vessel, its timbers blazing around the ammunition magazine, Maj. Barney put the fire out and towed the barge into shallow water. Fighting ended with the British squadron taking shelter under a large schooner's guns.

After two more similar skirmishes, 9 and 11 June, Barney found that two British frigates had effectively bottled up his flotilla in St. Leonard's Creek. To help him shake loose, the Navy Secretary sent Captain Samuel Miller with 100 marines and three pieces of cannon, and the War Secretary sent Colonel Decius Wadsworth with two 18-pounders and the support of 600 regular troops.

A joint breakout effort, with guns in a battery on a commanding height near the creek's mouth and the fleet in three divisions moving down on the blockading frigates, took place at dawn 26 June. The gunboats braved a rain of grape and canister shot. Despite failure of the battery to support effectively—due to "a great many blunders"—Barney's boats battled for nearly an hour, losing four killed and seven wounded.

Fought bravely and skillfully, the action proved that gunboats could not cope with the British Chesapeake fleet.

Com. Barney made no further attempt to take the flotilla out. On 1 July he went to Washington to talk over its future and to give his views on protecting the Chesapeake from ruinous British attacks. For on 27 June President Madison and his Cabinet had met in a gloomy session of defeat. From American peace commissioners in Europe had come word that Great Britain, having put Napoleon in his place, now assembled armies at Montreal and Bermuda to reduce America to a fit state of subjugation.

The American army stood defensively on the Canadian border, all hope of conquering Canada long since abandoned; the American Navy, despite derring-do on the high seas, could not defend her own coast; the nation's import revenues had fallen to almost nothing; her treasury lay bare.

That same day the Secretary of State wrote the peace commissioners to agree, if necessary, to a treaty without stipulations regarding impressment—in effect, surrender.

2

FROM TANGIER ISLAND where he awaited Cochrane's arrival from Bermuda with British invasion troops, Cockburn spent the spring and early summer raiding in the Potomac, some 10 miles across from Tangier Sound, and the Patuxent, some 20 miles above the Potomac. Reports reaching Washington and Baltimore, blockaded from Tangier, told of Cockburn's wanton destructiveness along the shores of both rivers and capture of Maryland tobacco worth $1,500,000.

Midshipman William Stanhope Lovell of frigate *Severn*, 44, describes how the British spent 17 July until 17 August "attacking and, to use an American expression, 'scaring the militia,' getting fresh provisions, destroying their storehouses and other public buildings with the arms found there.

"Some of the Americans used to say," he reports, with a poor ear for the colloquial, " 'What did King George send you here from the old country to come and scare us for? We don't go to yours to frighten you, I guess. Your confounded sarpents come and anchor in our waters; then send their barges, full of armed men, who are pulling about day and night, landing here and there, scaring us and our families very considerably—tarnation seize them.' Our reply used to be, 'You must ask your President, Jim Madison: he invited us.' "

The midshipman also tells of embarking from 1,500 to 2,000 slaves.

"The young men we formed into a black corps and . . . drilled and endeavoured to make our recruits of some use. The aged men, with the women and children, were sent to Halifax, Nova Scotia, and from thence a free colony was formed at the island of Trinidada, in the West Indies."

But an American prisoner in the Bahamas, one Captain Williams, in a sworn affidavit presented to the United States Senate, affirmed that he witnessed a Bahama sale of Negroes taken from the vicinity of Norfolk and Hampton.

Another sensitive British midshipman, Frederick Chamier, arriving in the Chesapeake "amid that general war of conflagration and devastation which half ruined the fertile shores of Virginia and Maryland," viewed Cockburn's activities closely from frigate *Menelaus*, 38, and pictures the scene like this:

"Because forsooth some savages, or perhaps men dressed one degree better than savages, commence a system of barbarity and desolation in the north, we, pretending to be the most civilized nation on the face of the earth, must imitate their ravages in the south; because, in Canada, some huts and hovels were burnt, we in the Chesapeake were to burn and destroy some noble mansion, desolate some magnificent estate, and turn a land of plenty and prosperity into a bleak desert of starvation and misery."

From constant practice, this perceptive sailor relates with his tongue in his cheek, Cockburn's raiders became "most consummately skilled in the art of house-burning. It is quite a mistake to set fire to a house to windward; it should always be fired to the leeward side; the air becoming rarified by the heat, the wind rushes round the corners and blows the flames against the house; whereas, on the weather side, the wind blows the flames round the angles, one half of their force is lost, and consequently time is consumed as well as the house.

". . . we tried the effect on two houses at the same time;

and it was admitted, even by the owners who had been guilty of the gross inconsistency and folly of defending their native land, that 'the firing to leeward' was equally as efficacious, and doubly as expeditious."

With similar candor:

"It has been held by many very good and clever men that, during war, private property should be respected: this is a very great mistake. Every man during war pays something towards the support of it: if this man is ruined, he ceases to contribute, and thus the exchequer is impoverished; ergo, the more you ruin in a war, the more you hurt the nation at large.

"But sometimes, and the American war was a proof of it, the greatest inconsistencies existed: for instance, we never were allowed to take cattle without paying for them. A bullock was estimated at five dollars, although it was worth twenty; and sheep had the high price of one dollar attached to them, they being in reality worth six at least. Yet did we burn the house of the man to whom the stock belonged.

"But supposing, and I have seen it one hundred times, that the farmer refused the money for his stock; why then we drove sheep, bullocks, and geese away, and left the money for the good man to take afterwards—as Quakers leave their taxes, which they have foresworn not to pay.

"I should like to have explained why we, sharks as we were, swallowed up every little schooner laden with fruit, or with ducks, etc., going to market; and why we were made to pay for the same articles if we found them on shore. The hue and cry always was 'Respect private property': 'Pay for what you take but take care to take all you can': and under this wholesale legislation we burnt and destroyed right and left.

"If by any stretch of argument we could establish the owner of a house, cottage, hut, etc. to be a militiaman, that house we burnt, because we found arms therein; that is to say, we found a duck gun, or a rifle. It so happens, that in America every man must belong to the militia; and, consequently, every man's house was food for a bonfire. And so well did we act up to the very spirit of our orders, that if the Americans who bounded the shores of Virginia and Maryland do not entail upon their posterities the deepest hatred and the loudest curses upon England and her marauders, why, they must possess more Christian charity than I give them credit for. . . .

"The ruin, the desolation, the heartless misery that we left them to brood over will forever make the citizens of the United States, in spite of the relationships of the countries, hate us with that hatred which no words can allay, or time eradicate."

Nature on occasion took a hand at chastening the invaders when helpless American householders could not. Observing that "some parts of this coast are subject to tornadoes," Midshipman Lovell tells about his frigate having to let go a second anchor when such a big blow struck 25 July.

"The previous day and that morning had been extremely sultry. The storm came on from the northwest, with the greatest violence, accompanied by a few claps of thunder and vivid flashes of lightning; such was its force that, although in smooth water, the ship heeled so much over that our main-deck guns nearly touched the water; and a fine schooner of 70 tons burthen, tender to *Severn*, with a long 18-pounder on board, at anchor near us without topmasts, her sails furled and gaffs on deck, was turned bottom upwards in a moment, and one poor fellow drowned.

"Its fury was spent in about ten minutes, but during its continuance we saw immense trees torn up by the roots, barns blown down like card houses of children and, where the strength of the current of wind passed, scarcely anything could withstand its violence.

"Trees and other things continued to be swept by us for some time, and when the tornado was over we observed, at a turn of the river, so much large timber, lumber, and other articles floating down the tide that my gallant senior officer,

Captain Joseph Nourse, thought at first it was the American flotilla coming to attack us, and he was just on the point of returning to his ship to prepare for a fight, he having come on board to dine with me, when I discovered, by means of a spy-glass, the approaching flotilla was perfectly harmless."

Defections and sickness plagued Cockburn until it hurt. The coxswain and ten young and healthy English and Scottish oarsmen of 74-gun *Albion*'s first cutter—the admiral's barge—sent to Watts Island to cut spars and stakes for the battery on Tangier Island, deserted and sold the barge with oars and sails complete for $50 to Lieutenant-Colonel Thomas Bayley commanding at Camp Chessenessix where the deserters reported that:

". . . crews are very sickly with the flux, the water being brackish and bad—they had been for two months on short allowance of food. . . ."

Tangier's fort had only three sides done, each side 259 yards long, mounting eight 24-pounders and about to mount twelve 24-pounders; but the island's gardens had vegetables of all kinds growing; the island also had a church, twenty houses built and laid out in streets, and a hospital to contain 100 sick.

Inexorably, Cockburn continued his harassment in the Potomac and, every time he landed, American defenders fell back. Upriver on the Maryland side, his men ran wild.

"I passed through Chaptico shortly after the enemy left," one outraged citizen reported, with the corroboration of Brigadier-General Philip Stuart commanding there, "and I am sorry to say that their conduct would have disgraced cannibals. The houses were torn to pieces, the well which afforded water for the inhabitants was filled up and, what was still worse, the church and the ashes of the dead suffered an equally bad or worse fate. Will you believe me when I tell you that the sunken graves were converted into barbacue holes?"

Downriver, Cockburn plundered the Potomac's Virginia side in the Yeocomico and Coan Rivers.

Altogether, he thoroughly scared the militia, and the inhabitants, of both states while he waited for Cochrane, in Bermuda, to assemble the naval and military forces for Britain's major amphibious attack in the Chesapeake.

3

THE BRITISH land forces destined for the invasion of the United States under Major-General Robert Ross took ship in France's Garonne River on 2 June. Wellington veterans like Gen. Ross, they wore their campaign-battered, plumed black shakos and faded scarlet coats with blue facings.

As reported on the spot by eighteen-year-old Subaltern George Robert Gleig of the Eighty-fifth Regiment, the army consisted of:

"... three battalions of infantry, the Fourth, Forty-fourth, and Eighty-fifth Regiments; the two former mustering each about 800 bayonets, the last not more than 600.

"In addition to these, there were two officers of engineers, a brigade of artillery, a detachment of sappers and miners, a party of artillery drivers, with a due proportion of officers belonging to the Medical and Commissariat departments. The whole together could not be computed at more than 2,500 men, if indeed it amounted to so great a number; and was placed under the command of Major-General Ross, a very gallant and experienced officer."

Forty-eight-year-old Robert Ross—of an Irish family with seat at Rosstrevor, County Down—had shown his gallantry and gained his experience in Holland, Egypt, Italy, Portugal, Spain, and France.

Easy-mannered, dignified, and humane as well as brave, he held the hearts of his men and their officers despite his insistence on rigid discipline and relentless drill. Having begun his career during the American Revolution, he had learned skirmishing tactics; he had practiced them against Napoleon.

On the Peninsula's snowy mountains and frozen roads, Ross had had the warm companionship of his courageous Irish wife. Leaving her when he took ship for America, he told her that he sailed on his last campaign.

The British fleet consisted of: *Royal Oak*, 74 guns, bearing the flag of Rear-Admiral Poulteney Malcolm; *Diadem* and *Dictator*, 64's, armed *en flûte* (lower-deck guns taken out, to make room for troops); *Pomone*, *Menelaus*, *Trave*, *Weser*, and *Thames*, frigates—the last three armed in the same manner as *Diadem* and *Dictator*; *Meteor* and *Devastation*, bomb vessels which carried rocket-launching tubes and mortars for hurling explosive shells; together with one or two gun-brigs —making in all a squadron of eleven or twelve warships, with several store-ships and transports.

Following a stopover at St. Michael's in the Azores, the voyage to Bermuda took from 27 June to 24 July, almost an entire month at sea; a long time on shipboard to maintain troop morale. Besides the amusements which nature supplied —watching porpoises, looking at sea and sky—Lieut. Gleig reports that officers gave balls and other public entertainments through the fleet as often as weather permitted.

"On the 19th of July at an early hour in the morning a signal was made from the *Royal Oak* that the admiral would be happy to see the officers of the fleet on board his ship that evening. Boats were accordingly sent off from the different vessels, loaded with visitors; and, on mounting the gangway, a stage with a green curtain before it was discovered on the quarterdeck.

"The whole of the deck, from the poop to the mainmast, was hung round with flags so as to form a moderate sized theatre; and the carronades were removed from their portholes in order to make room for the company. Lamps were suspended from all parts of the rigging and shrouds, casting a brilliant light upon this singular playhouse; and the crew, arranged in their best attire, crowded the booms, yards, and fore part of the deck; whilst the space from the mainmast to the foot of the stage was set with benches for the more genteel part of the audience."

At 7 P.M., the curtain went up, to reveal a scene "painted with such taste as would not have disgraced any theatre in London." The play, *The Apprentice*, with *The Mayor of Garret* as afterpiece, was performed by officers of the ship and the artillery.

"To witness a comedy and a farce upon that stage, and in the middle of the Atlantic Ocean," Lieut. Gleig declares, "was delightful for its very singularity."

When the performance ended, seamen took the stage down and cleared the deck for dancing.

"The music was excellent," the lieutenant reports, "being composed of the band of the *Royal Oak;* and the ball was opened by Admiral Malcolm and the Honourable Mrs. Mullens [no doubt traveling with army and navy wives to Bermuda and Halifax] in a country dance, followed by as many couples as the space would permit; the greater number of officers dancing, as necessity required, with one another."

From admiral and general down to youngest midshipman and subaltern, everyone laid aside "all restraint or form of discipline" and filled the night with spirits until 12 P.M. when a blue light went up the flagship's hoist to signal boats to take visitors back to their ships.

On the evening of 29 July, a second squadron from the Mediterranean appeared off Bermuda bringing Twenty-first Royal Scots Fusileers, mustering 900 bayonets, to join Ross.

"By this very acceptable reinforcement," says Lieut. Gleig, "our numbers were increased to upwards of 3,000 effective men, and a greater confidence in themselves, as well as a better grounded hope of success in whatever they might undertake, was at the same time given to the troops."

On 3 August, the invasion army once more got under way, the British fleet standing towards America. Gen. Ross raced ahead with Cochrane in 80-gun flagship *Tonnant,* which had

flown the French flag before Nelson captured her in the battle
of the Nile, to confer with Cockburn.

Towards evening eleven days later, Adm. Malcolm anchored his squadron for the night off the capes. And when
dawn of 15 August broke the British again hoisted sail "and
stood in gallant style up the Chesapeake."

Immediately on entering, Lieut. Gleig reports, "we were
joined by Admiral Cockburn with three line-of-battle ships,
several frigates and a few sloops of war and gun-brigs, by
which means the squadron could now muster above twenty
vessels entitled to display the pendant, besides an equal if not
a greater number of victuallers and transports."

By Lieut. Gleig's calculations, the British counted on landing a corps of at least 4,000 men.

"The spectacle was therefore as agreeable and imposing as
might be," the young lieutenant excitedly wrote, "because we
could not help remembering that this magnificent fleet was
sailing in an enemy's bay, and that it was filled with troops
for the invasion of that enemy's country. Thus, like a snow-
ball, we had gathered as we went on and, from having set
out a mere handful of soldiers, were now become an army
formidable as well from its numbers as its discipline."

Shoals and sandbanks encumbering navigation, the ships
anchored every night. Their first day's sail carried them only
to the mouth of the James River; their second to the mouth
of the Potomac where they stayed the night of 17 August
and a considerable part of the following day. On 18 August
they moved toward the mouth of the Patuxent River, a storm
threatening, and that evening, clouds dispersed and water
again like a glass lake, prepared for the invasion.

4

WHEN COCHRANE and Ross arrived from Bermuda and joined
Cockburn on 12 August at the mouth of the Potomac, ther-
mometers registered 103 degrees on *Tonnant*'s deck, 82 de-

grees below decks, and 82½ degrees in the water. Dining on vegetables fresh from Tangier Island's gardens and turtles fresh from Chesapeake Bay, the trio thrashed out invasion plans.

On 1 July Cochrane had sent Cockburn, top secret, his ideas for action in the Chesapeake—beginning with an attack on Washington. To Earl Bathurst, Secretary of State for War and the Colonies, he explained on 14 July that this would forward the over-all British plan of diverting American attention from Canada where British troops gathered for a thrust down Lake Champlain toward New York.

"I trust to be able to find the enemy free employment for all his troops in Virginia, Maryland and Pennsylvania, without detaching them to the Canadian Frontier," Cochrane wrote Bathurst. "If [British] troops arrive soon and the point of attack is directed toward Baltimore, I have every prospect of success and Washington will be equally accessible. They may be destroyed or laid under contribution, as the occasion may require. . . .

"I have much at heart to give them a good drubbing before peace is made."

Cockburn on 17 July enthusiastically suggested in detail how to carry out these plans. He proposed disembarking British troops at the town of Benedict on the Patuxent, about 35 miles from Washington as the crow flew, 50 as soldiers marched. From Benedict a hilly highroad passed through Piscataway, 4 miles from Fort Washington which offered the only hindrance to a march on the American capital.

"I therefore most firmly believe," Cockburn declared, "that within forty-eight hours after arrival in the Patuxent of such a force as you expect, the city of Washington might be possessed without difficulty or opposition of any kind."

Ships of the fleet, Cockburn pointed out, could cover a landing at Benedict, and smoothness of the water in the river would render them entirely independent of the weather. Too, rich country around Benedict would afford necessary immediate supplies and horses to transport cannons.

To lull the Americans into a feeling of security along the Patuxent, Cockburn had withdrawn to feint along the Potomac. He felt confident that everything would remain exactly as he left it until the invasion.

He wrote Cochrane: "The facility and rapidity, after its being first discovered, with which an army by landing at Benedict might possess itself of the Capital, always so great a blow to the Government of a country, as well on account of the resources of the documents and records the invading army is almost sure to obtain thereby, must strongly, I should think, urge the propriety of the plan, and the more particularly as the other places you have mentioned will be more likely to fall after the occupation of Washington, than that city would be after their capture."

He reminded Cochrane that Americans always had felt that any attack on Washington would come via Annapolis; but that the shallow water at Annapolis, tolerably well fortified, would offer problems for large British ships. He pointed out, also, that Baltimore posed difficulties for ships drawing more than 16 feet of water; they could approach only within 7 or 8 miles of the Patapsco's mouth.

He therefore strongly recommended that, if Cochrane, too, deemed Washington worthy of first efforts, "our main forces should be landed in the Patuxent, yet a tolerable good division should at the same time be sent up the Potowmac with bomb ships, etc., which will tend to distract and divide the enemy, amuse Fort Washington if it does not reduce it, and will probably offer other advantages of importance without any counter-balancing inconvenience, as the communication between the grand army and this division will be easy and immediate in consequence of the very small space between the Potowmac and the Patuxent."

Cockburn already had a pilot for the rivers and a guide for the roads—an American "who has been ill-treated in his

own country and seems extremely anxious to be revenged"
—and would not find it difficult to obtain more such men
"when we have force to protect them and money to pay
them."

As he detailed his ideas in person to Cochrane and Ross
that hot 12 August, Cockburn pointed out how profitably he
had spent his time while awaiting the invasion army. His raids
had destroyed military stores established in Virginia and
Maryland to clothe and arm American forces, harassed troops
intended for protection of the capital, and misled the American people "as to the true and ultimate point of attack."

Too, his feint up the Potomac had ascertained the passage
past Kettle Bottom shoals and inclined numerous Negroes to
join the British.

Cochrane liked this last. Having ordered horses collected,
he would put Negroes into the saddle. As he had informed
Bathurst, Negroes could be made "as good Cossacks as any
in the Russian army, and more terrific to the Americans than
any troops that can be brought forward." He could use them
handily in his campaign of retaliation.

Governor Prevost of Canada having advised him that
American troops had burned the town of Dover 14 May in
reported reprisal for the burning of Havre de Grace, Cochrane
had told his north Atlantic fleet:

"You will hold strictly in view the conduct of the American Army toward His Majesty's unoffending Canadian sub-
jects, and you will spare merely the lives of the unarmed
American inhabitants in the United States. For only by carrying this retaliation into the country of the enemy can we
hope to make him sensible of the impolicy as well as the
inhumanity of the system he has adopted."

He righteously added:

"You will take every opportunity of explaining to the people how much I lament the necessity of following the rigorous
example of the American forces."

To give Gen. Ross a feel of the American countryside in

which he would carry out that policy, Cockburn took the British general to burn a factory back of St. George Island and, 16 August, the three top commanders conferred with fleet officers on final invasion plans.

They discarded Cockburn's suggestion of marching on Washington by way of Piscataway and the left bank of the Potomac, for two reasons: (1) in order to take care of Com. Barney's flotilla in the Patuxent, and (2) to avoid having to cross the Potomac's Eastern Branch outside the capital via either of its bridges. The invaders would land at Benedict as Cockburn recommended, but march on Washington along the Patuxent's right bank to Bladensburg where the Eastern Branch could be forded.

This plan had merit. As Cochrane reported to the Admiralty, Barney's flotilla "afforded a pretext for ascending the river to attack him nearer its sources . . . while the ultimate destination of the combined forces was Washington, should it be found that the attempt might be made with any prospect of success."

As America's darkest day drew near, Cochrane on 17 August sent Captain James Alexander Gordon in frigate *Sea Horse*, 38, up the Potomac with six other vessels including bomb ships whose mortars could hurl explosive shells more than 2 miles. Capt. Gordon sailed toward Alexandria "with a view of destroying Fort Washington and opening a free communication above, as well as to cover the retreat of the army from Washington."

That same day, Captain Peter Parker's frigate *Menelaus* led several smaller vessels toward the head of Chesapeake Bay "to divert the enemy in that quarter."

Britain's main invasion fleet, thirty-eight sail, left the Potomac's mouth, entered the Patuxent and, on the evening of 18 August when the larger ships "took ground," came to anchor about 2 miles below Benedict.

5

To ESTABLISH a modern Rome in the new world, England's eccentric Francis Pope in 1663 bought a tract of land where the Potomac River forked, gave the name Tiber to one of its creeks, and called a nearby elevation Capitoline Hill. One hundred and twenty-seven years later, 16 July 1790, America's President George Washington signed a congressional bill locating the new nation's Federal City on this and additional Maryland and Virginia land and authorized the District of Columbia's first map.

Foreigners as well as United States citizens bought lots in the 7,100-acre "city in the woods" whose grand plan of broad streets, with avenues up to 160 feet wide, came from the creative mind of thirty-seven-year-old Major Pierre Charles L'Enfant. Engineer son of an applied artist and tapestry maker, L'Enfant had followed Lafayette from France to fight in the American Revolution.

George Washington approving, L'Enfant and Andrew Ellicott carefully located two grand edifices to "command the greatest prospect and be susceptible of the greatest improvement." They planned "Congress House," ninety feet above the Potomac on Jenkins Hill, with a "dome beautiful in all phases of the atmosphere and the surrounding landscape." To form a vista down Pennsylvania Avenue, they planned the "President's House."

For the Capitol, George Washington wanted a combination of grandeur, simplicity, and convenience. Thomas Jefferson wanted a building simple, noble, beautiful. But the first competition brought no plan worthy of their aims. They had encouraged one of the architects to try again when, from the West Indies, came the letter of an English-born Virgin Islander educated in Edinburgh and Paris. Dr. William Thornton, honeymooning in his birthplace after living in America, asked if he might try.

Dr. Thornton's design, admired by both Washington and

Jefferson, won the approval of Commissioners Thomas John-
son and Daniel Carroll of Maryland and David Stuart of
Virginia, in charge of laying out the Federal City. And on
18 September 1793, thirteenth year of American independence,
George Washington laid the Capitol's cornerstone to the gala
accompaniment of artillery volleys and a 500-pound barbe-
cued ox.

Captain Samuel Smallwood's quarries in nearby Rock
Creek furnished Congress House's foundation stone, hard
brick formed its inner walls, and its facing of freestone came
from the banks of the Potomac. Its completed north wing
greeted the Senate when President John Adams opened the
Sixth Congress 17 November 1800; House members, their
wing not ready, used space later made into the first Library
of Congress.

The President's House went up on a second eminence
overlooking the river, a mile and a half distant from the Capitol because George Washington had found in New York and
Philadelphia that propinquity of President and legislators re-
tarded business and consumed time.

Designed and called the "President's Palace" by James
Hoban, an Irish medal man of the Dublin Society of Arts,
the President's House looked like a gentleman's home of the
period, a good period. Set in a tract of 80 acres which encom-
passed an undrained swamp with frogs, crows, and wolves, it
had a rough wood fence to separate it from Colonel John B.
Tayloe's racetrack.

Hoban's only design success in forty-two years of government service, the two-story presidential mansion whose high
basement gave a third story to its southern exposure had facings of Aquia Creek sandstone. Of high brilliance, this Virginia stone cut freely in any direction without splitting; it
had a reddish-yellow hue, coarse grain, and many imbedded
white pebbles. The mansion's cornerstone went into place
just 300 years after America's discovery, 13 October 1792.

When John and Abigail Adams took possession in 1800

they could use only six of its rooms. They had no bathroom. Water came into the mansion, hauled by hand, from Franklin Park five city blocks away.

Besides having two wells dug, Thomas Jefferson built a bowerlike one-story structure to handle office work away from the mansion and, between the two, put up meat house, wine cellar, coal and wood sheds, and privies. On the mansion's opposite side, he erected horse and carriage barns and a cowshed. To the house itself, Jefferson gave character that endured.

In 1809 James and Dolly* Madison added a touch of fashion—yellow satin upholstery, satin damask draperies on windows, mirrors over mantelpieces, a $458 piano, and a $28 guitar. In the dining room, visiting Elbridge Gerry, Jr. found General Washington "represented as large as life" in a full-length portrait.

From the second story's circular room, Dolly Madison had a very extended and magnificent view of the Potomac. "On a clear day," she wrote, "the distant points of Fort Washington may be dimly defined, and the old city of Georgetown distinctly seen." From this room she also could view the town of Alexandria on the farther side of Long Bridge, a mile southwest of the mansion. She could not see the Potomac's mouth, 75 bee-line miles away and almost 100 via the river itself, nor Baltimore some 40 miles in the opposite direction.

The city of Washington had no paving, no water system, no drainage. Instead of extending from a central point, it straggled over 3 to 4 square miles and sprouted in twenty or thirty different places without sign of business or industry. In 1800 its inventory listed 109 brick buildings, 263 wood buildings, and 3,000 population. Georgetown had 5,000, Alexandria 3,000.

When the federal government moved all departments except the Treasury, with sixty-nine employes, from Philadelphia 11 June that year, State brought seven employes, War brought

---

* See Notes, Chap. III.

eighteen, Navy fifteen, Post Office nine, plus thirteen not attached to any department at an estimated moving cost of $15,293 above $32,872 expenses for employes' families. State papers traveled by water, private effects by road. The federal offices located in the capital at scattered points, according to L'Enfant's original plan.

Pennsylvania Avenue, connecting Congress House and the President's House, had down its middle a roadway, ordered in 1792, of "a breadth of two perches." In 1800 this 32-foot track looked like nothing more than "a deep morass covered with elderbushes," and wood choppers still cleared forest trees on it.

Jefferson divided the avenue into three lanes bordered by four rows of Lombardy poplars, and rode on it to his second inaugural address in the Senate. But guests at the few abutting houses often had to have their carriages driven onto the narrow footpath outside the poplars in order to step onto the brick path of their host's residence. A ditch between the poplars often filled with stagnant water, and in wet weather callers found the avenue all mud; in dry weather, all dust.

Over the years much of the city's forest went for fuel, although a visitor observed that enough trees stood "for shooting grounds to amuse those addicted to sport of the field." He noted also that of the population "probably one-half are blacks and most of the remainder members of congress, clerks, servants, innkeepers, or in some way appurtenant to the government." Wrote another: "The barber who shaves me of a morning comes on horseback with his razors; and the physician . . . lives five miles from my lodgings."

By 1813, the Federal City had nearly 9,000 population according to Joseph Gales's *National Intelligencer*, though rival *Richmond Inquirer* lowered the figure to "little more than 8,000." In August, September, and October one adult died of old age, while four succumbed to dysentery, and six adults and four children died of cholera. A doctor reported in the paper, following that summer which Madison for-

tunately survived, "low grounds west of the Capitol which
were formerly the grand source of our autumnal fevers, have
been completely drained by means of the canal; and the once
stagnant waters of this marsh are now happily converted into
the waters of the Potomac. The citizens of Washington have
enjoyed a great share of health during the last summer."

By now Washington's Capitol brought praise from all sides.
Wrote an English admirer: "In no part of the world are there
more noble edifices devoted to similar purposes . . . the Hall
of the Representatives is of spacious dimensions; an oval, surrounded by twenty-four Corinthian pillars, and surmounted
by a lofty, painted dome, through which the light is admitted
by a hundred apertures . . . the furniture, decorations and arrangement are becoming and elegant; and during a night
session, when the hall is lighted by lamps, the whole effect is
fine and imposing.

"The Senate chamber is in the other wing . . . with a
double-arched dome, and Ionic pillars; the drapery, hangings
and carpets, and indeed the whole chamber, finished in a
superior style of splendour and brilliancy. Under the Senate
chamber is the Hall of Justice.

"The main body of the Capitol has not been begun, and
all these halls are in the wings. The whole pile, when completed, will be enormous. The vestibules, stairways, and galleries of communications are designed and executed with great
magnificence." A far cry from Upper Canada's brick-walled
wood capitol!

Since 1811, with war impending, Congress had stopped
appropriating for public buildings. As a result, the magnificent
Capitol, standing on a steep declivity covered with ancient
oaks and looking over many gullies and few buildings to the
Navy Yard, had its two imposing wings connected only by a
rough-board corridor across the central portion's finished
foundation.

Despite forlorn surroundings—grounds, sidewalks and
driveways uncared for, even not yet laid down—it continued

to attract active, reflective, and ambitious citizens of Washington, men and women from every state of the union, and notable foreigners.

The Hall of Representatives served as a gathering place for all those "whom fashion, fame, beauty, wealth or talents have render'd celebrated." It served, too, for Sunday congregation. But the gay groups that assembled from Georgetown and environs to hear distinguished visiting clergymen preach made the occasion more fashionable than religious.

"The members of Congress gladly gave up their seats for such fair auditors," a regular attendant records, "and either lounged in the lobbies, or round the fireplaces, or stood beside the ladies of their acquaintance. This sabbath-day resort became so fashionable that the floor of the house offered insufficient space; the platform behind the Speaker's chair and every spot where a chair could be wedged in was crowded with ladies in their gayest costume and their attendant beaux who led them to their seats with the same gallantry as exhibited in a ballroom.

"Smiles, nods, whispers, nay sometimes tittering, marked their recognition of each other and beguiled the tedium of the service. Often, when cold, a lady would leave her seat and, led by her attending beau, would make her way through the crowd to one of the fireplaces where she could laugh and talk at her ease.

"One of the officers of the House, followed by his attendant with a great bag over his shoulder, precisely at 12 o'clock would make his way through the hall to the depository of letters to put them in the mailbag, which sometimes had a most ludicrous effect and always diverted attention from the preacher.

"The musick was as little in union with devotional feelings as the place. The Marine band were the performers. Their scarlet uniform, their various instruments, made quite a dazzling appearance in the gallery. The marches they played were good and inspiring, but in their attempts to accompany the psalm-singing of the congregation they completely failed and after a while the practice was discontinued—it was *too* ridiculous." During his entire administration, Jefferson attended regularly.

Seen through a foreigner's eyes, Washington's gaiety presented a wild and somewhat woolly appearance, especially horse racing "to which Americans are much addicted." Held in a large open field such as Tayloe's track, races attracted "a tumultuous concourse of men, horses and carriages."

The races collected together, as a Greek visitor wrote home, "persons of all descriptions from the President and his chief officers of state down to their Negro slaves, driving pell-mell about the route, shouting, betting, drinking, quarreling and fighting. Booths and tents were erected, in some of which refreshments were offered for sale and in others gambling tables were kept, and stages on which the judges of the course were mounted.

"You must not be astonished," he went on, "at hearing that a number of beautiful females were present, sitting exposed on the tops and boxes of carriages, and in other conspicuous seats. Every line of separation is so entirely obliterated that wherever there are men you may be sure to meet women, in this country; and for my own part, I have no doubt that the women in the end will ride uppermost."

What with horses neighing, bettors shouting, drinkers clinking their glasses and quarreling, the uproar fascinated the visitor. As for the race itself!

"Such horses and such a contest! Instead of noble rampant animals, bearing their crest aloft and pawing the ground, all pride, phrensy and ambition, a couple of miserable skeletons crawled tamely up to the goal; for in this perverse country, it seems, they reduce instead of pampering their cattle for a race, and for four and twenty hours beforehand allow them nothing to eat.

"The riders were dressed in parti-colored clothes, with spurs on their heels and whips in their hands, to excite the sorry beasts they rode . . . the battered brutes bled faster than they ran. . . ."

Riding home after the race, the visitor in his hackney coach crept along the highway in a traffic jam of horsemen, hikers, chaises, stages, and carts. And his day's adventures were rounded out with a storm that blew, he said, like an Arabian sirocco.

"I experienced many a gale at sea, but never such a land breeze as this. The horses could hardly stem it. The old coach creaked to the blast. The coachman lashed with all his might—but in vain—the tempest was irresistible; and we were blown, horses, hack, and all, off the road into a deep ditch at the side, where I lay till the horses were cut loose from the harness and the door loosened from the hinges . . . a flash of sharp lightning, followed by a peal of thunder . . . torrents of rain, with continued streams of lightning and peals of thunder. . . ."

Despite the fact that the British fleet hovered in the Chesapeake, Washington in 1813 generally believed that the enemy could not ascend the Potomac. Weddings, dinners, assemblies, glittering embassy functions, and Navy Yard balls at which the newly introduced waltz proved the season's sensation kept the capital's citizens from brooding.

During this time, Cockburn held his finger on the pulse of American feeling. British officers in disguise,* and Americans in the pay of the British, frequented the city's hotels and passed in and out of the capital unquestioned. Too, Cockburn received the District's newspapers almost as regularly as any local subscriber. He worked up a particular hate for the *National Intelligencer,* which closely reflected the American government's views.

While Dolly Madison tended her sick husband that summer, she sensed impending danger. Writing to the President's secretary just before Madison fell ill, she told Edward Coles of efforts to prepare Fort Washington for a possible British attack via the Potomac and informed him that, though a

* See Notes, Chap. III.

Quaker, she always had advocated fighting when assailed and therefore kept "the old Tunisian sabre within reach."

She added a report of British plans "to land as many chosen rogues as they can about fourteen miles below Alexandria, in the night, so that they may be on hand to burn the President's House and offices." She wrote: "I do not tremble at this, but feel hurt that the admiral (of Havre de Grace memory) should send me word that he would make his bow at my drawing-room very soon."

6

WHEN 1813 invasion threats faded, Washington rocked back to sleep. A citizen's committee, formed to reorganize the District militia, suspended activities. And a brilliant Congress House reception opened the new year of 1814.

The capital—hill-encircled and, in General Washington's opinion, admirably situated for defense—stood virtually unprotected, without even a warning system of outposts. Downriver, Fort Washington and a few troops could hardly defend the entire city.

Nor could the naval force which Secretary Jones had pulled together: three 18-pounders and four 24-pounders on ships' carriages behind a breastwork on Greenleaf Point near the Eastern Branch's juncture with the Potomac; three scows moored with carronades below the Navy Yard to rake the channel; a mobile barge with two 12-pound carronades.

In the Yard itself the Marine Guard—fixed in 1806 at one captain, two lieutenants, four musicians, three sergeants, two corporals, and 45 privates—had more than they could do to cope with "nocturnal depredations" that lifted Navy pork over the east wall.

Congress voted down resolutions to place the capital in a defensive state, and the Secretary of War—Brigadier-General John Armstrong—kept his sights set on invading Canada.

Long-faced, long-nosed, with a high forehead, Armstrong

had a reputation for indolence, an inability to work harmoniously with others, and many enemies. With his anonymous "Newburgh Addresses" of 1783, he had called for a mutiny of Continental Army officers. The British Minister in 1804 had set down that he was "regarded as an artful man, of tolerably good talents, and perfectly without principle." Madison distrusted him.

Yet, he had served in the United States Senate, gone to France as American Minister, and won congressional confirmation—though by a grudging 18 votes to 15—as Secretary of War. He took office 5 February 1813. Since then he had overlooked Washington's defense while focusing his gaze on the Canadian border.

Madison and Monroe had pressed Armstrong to make adequate preparations to defend the capital, as did Major-General John P. Van Ness, prominent Washington banker who commanded the District's militia of two brigades. In June, the War Secretary reported 2,154 troops available—scattered from Baltimore to Norfolk.

Out of its fateful 1 July deliberations, the Cabinet brought forth a plan to defend Washington with an army from all eighteen states. Although the bulk of these men would remain subject to call, portions of the quotas from three neighboring states—Maryland, 6,000; Virginia, 2,000; Pennsylvania, 5,000—would take immediate position between Baltimore and the Potomac. With the District militia and companies of regular infantry and troops of dragoons, they would constitute a corps of some 2,000 to 3,000 disposable at all times under direction of the commanding general.

The plan left the capital dependent for security upon a citizen soldiery. And it entrusted the assembling of these soldiers to a War Secretary who did not believe the British had any intentions of moving on the city.

Next day, with creation of the Tenth Military Department —to comprise "the state of Maryland, the District of Columbia, and that part of Virginia lying between the Potomac and the Rappahannock"—Madison stimulated immediate action by selecting Brigadier-General William Henry Winder to command the new department.

War Secretary Armstrong took this appointment hard: he preferred Brigadier-General Moses Porter, a brave and experienced veteran of the Revolution and now commanding at Norfolk. Thereafter, Armstrong showed only the most passive interest in Washington's defense.

For the Navy, Com. Barney returned to his flagship *Scorpion*, thirteen barges, and 500 men in the Patuxent; his first lieutenant, Solomon Rutter, went to Baltimore to take over fourteen gunboats and 500 men stationed there.

Amid Fourth of July festivities, requisitions went to eighteen state governors for 93,500 soldiers, and, 5 July, fresh from a Baltimore oration, Brigadier-General Winder assumed his new duties.

The administration relaxed.

An amiable, captivating, handsome and successful Baltimore lawyer with a lieutenant-colonel's commission dated 16 March 1812, thirty-seven-year-old Winder had had the briefest of fighting experience—leading a successful expedition from Black Rock, near Buffalo, N. Y., to the Canadian shore below Fort Erie. Promoted brigadier-general 12 March 1813, he fell into British hands as hostage at the battle of Stoney Creek the following June. Exchanged, he had received appointment as an adjutant-general 9 May 1814, less than two months before Madison gave him command of the new Potomac district.

Trying to make up for Congress's lack of foresight in planning the capital's defense, Winder found himself frustrated by superiors. And with no staff—not even a secretary—he did his best to carry out the administration's ideas.

Like a good lawyer properly preparing a case for court, he went over his command territory, inspected forts, examined terrain, studied roads between the mouth of the Patuxent and the capital. He found his department without adequate provisions, forage, transport, tools, rifles, flints.

Returning to Washington, at the end of July he finally obtained a guard to turn random visitors from his office door while he wore himself out writing letters which produced no soldiers.

Because national and state governments shared responsibility for assembling militia forces, Winder ended up his frenetic exertions with only 250 Maryland militia, all his uncle the governor could send him from a call for 3,000. These comprised the sole force to reach him from outside the District of Columbia.

Probably no general ever found himself worse situated. Appointed to command an army, he led a corporal's guard under conditions that rendered his power nil.

On 1 August he had—in camp—about 1,000 Army regulars and—on call—some 4,000 local militia now under Brigadier-General Walter Smith of Georgetown. (Irked by President Madison's having put Winder over him, Gen. Van Ness the banker had resigned his commission.)

Winder's troops offered little promise. Mostly ill-trained farmers and tradesmen, these District militiamen lacked equipment, uniforms, and professional officers capable of military leadership. When they mustered into federal service in their motley dress and nondescript arms, Gen. Smith sent them back home for better shoes and told them, in effect, to bring a butcher knife if they couldn't lay hands on a musket.

Editor Gales of the *National Intelligencer* had had a hand in slowing down the capital's defense. Having taken the newspaper over in 1810 after three years as a reporter, with brother-in-law William W. Seaton as partner, he had raised the *Intelligencer* to the position of semiofficial presidential spokesman. Close observer of the Senate, Gales long had had a seat on the front rostrum, beside the Vice President's chair and, since the Senate had no official stenographer, had provided the Senate's principal record from his personal transcript.

Along with Madison (whom many British held personally responsible for taking the United States into the war), Gales

presented a target for enemy attack. Because in 1795 he had
fled from England with his father as a political refugee, his
life stood forfeit under British laws. Cockburn looked on
Gales, a naturalized American citizen, as a British traitor and
could not wait to get his hands on either him or his newspaper's type.

One Senator described Gales as standing "erect as the quills
on a porcupine," and Gales had tried valiantly to ward off
some of the condemnation heaped on Madison for permitting
British depredations in the Chesapeake area. Rather than arous-
ing fears of invasion, he had allayed them, emphatically playing down Washington's danger. In May the *Intelligencer* had
editorialized:

> What though the enemy has taken possession of some
> islands in the Chesapeake? It is absurd to suppose that
> government can fortify every point, island or nook along
> an extensive coast. The neighboring militia must protect
> them; and though their officers are principally federalists,
> yet they are not of the Boston stamp.
>
> Not long since one of our small privateers took pos-
> session of an island on the coast of Scotland, not perhaps
> one hundred miles from its capital, and held it for some
> weeks notwithstanding the tremendous naval and mili-
> tary force of Great Britain. Captain Porter with his
> small frigate [*Essex*] captured and fortified and long
> held possession of three islands in the Pacific.
>
> There is nothing, then, miraculous or alarming in the
> enemy's large fleet seizing and holding a few islands in
> the Chesapeake; in some of them erecting hospitals
> which, while he remains in our waters, we hope may be
> well filled. As to his near approach to the Capital, which
> has been hinted at, we have no idea of his attempting
> to reach this vicinity; and if he does, we have no doubt
> he will meet such a reception as he did at Craney Island.
> The enemy knows better what he is about than to trust
> himself abreast or on this side of Fort Washington.

Then, on the listless morning of Thursday, 18 August, a
dust-covered horseman galloped into the drowsing capital.

From Point Lookout, army observation post at the Potomac's mouth, he brought news that a massive British fleet had sailed into the Patuxent.

Capital reactions varied:

Indolent Secretary of War Armstrong told visiting banker Van Ness that the enemy "certainly will not come here." He added, "Baltimore is the place, sir," and did nothing. . . .

Winder called out the District militia . . . then scurried in and out of meetings. . . .

Federal department clerks packed up their records. . . .

Panicked citizens stacked personal belongings on doorsteps, and prepared to flee. . . .

Calling at the President's House during the morning, Secretary of State Monroe heard from Madison's lips of the enemy's approach to Benedict. As a Revolutionary War soldier with some experience of fighting the British, Colonel Monroe remarked that the city of Washington was their goal now. He offered "to proceed immediately to Benedict with a troop of horse to observe their force, report it, with my opinion of their objects, and, should they advance on this city, to retire before them, communicating regularly their movements to the government."

To this eminently practical proposal James Madison acceded.

4

DEBACLE
AT BLADENSBURG:
24 AUGUST 1814

I

FROM *Tonnant,* Cochrane directed the British landing at Benedict, first move in their fateful amphibious invasion of the United States. Cockburn commanded the naval force, Ross the troops.

Cockburn went about his part of the debarkation with his usual assurance. Ross—mannered gentleman, disciplined soldier —took his responsibility cautiously, according to his aide-de-camp Harry Smith. He "lacked that dashing enterprise essential to carry a place by a *coup de main.*"

The action of the British landing and the invaders' emotions as they came ashore to march toward Washington spring to life in the vivid narrative of curly-haired, round-faced Lieut. Gleig who recorded the scene as he experienced it. He begins on 18 August, with the fleet at the mouth of the Patuxent:

"There we lay, as we had done the day before, anxiously expecting a breeze; till about noon, the wind beginning to blow fair, the fleet entered the river and made its way slowly and majestically against the stream. The voyage soon became picturesque and interesting in the highest degree. Fields of Indian corn, with meadows of the most luxuriant pasture, stretched along the margin of the stream on either hand; whilst the neat wooden houses of the settlers, all painted white and surrounded with orchards and gardens, presented a striking contrast to the boundless forests which formed a background to the scene.

"Of the prodigious extent and gloomy appearance of these forests it is impossible for any language to convey an adequate conception. There is nothing, at least nothing which I have seen in the old world, at all resembling or to be compared with them. And hemming in, as they do on every side, the tiny spots of cultivation, they certainly convey no very enlarged idea of the power of human industry.

"The cleared fields on the banks of the Patuxent, for example, could in no direction measure above half a mile across —in many places their breadth fell short of that, from the river to the woods; and then all was one vast forest through which no eye could penetrate nor any traveller venture to seek his way. We were, as may be imagined, greatly taken by scenery so novel; and we continued to gaze upon it with the liveliest interest till our attention was drawn away to other and more important matters.

"We had not proceeded many miles from the river's mouth when a telegraph from the Admiral gave orders for the troops to be in readiness to land at a moment's notice. Everything was forthwith put in a state of forwardness: provisions for three days, that is to say, three pounds of pork, with two pounds and a half of biscuit, were cooked and given to the men; the cartouch-boxes were supplied with fresh ammunition, and the arms and accoutrements handed out.

"The fleet, however, continued to move on, without showing an inclination to bring to; till, at length having ascended to the distance of ten leagues from the Bay, the ships-of-the-line began to take ground; and, in a little while after, even the frigates could proceed no farther. But by this time the sun had

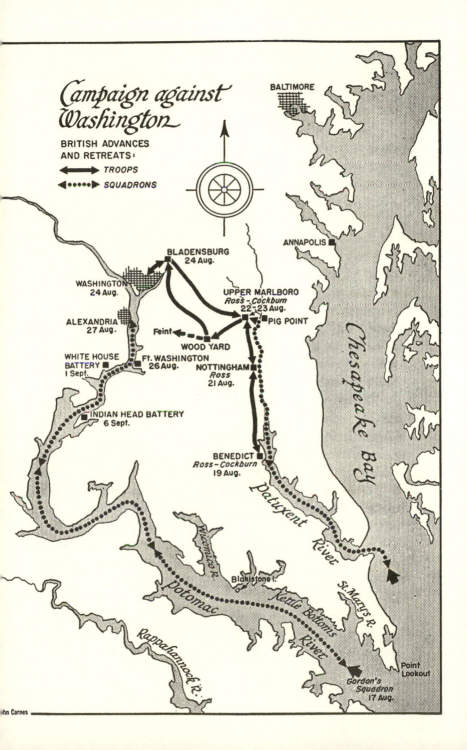

Campaign against Washington

BRITISH ADVANCES
AND RETREATS:

⬅━━━➡ TROOPS
◀•••••▶ SQUADRONS

BALTIMORE

ANNAPOLIS

BLADENSBURG
24 Aug.

WASHINGTON
24 Aug.

UPPER MARLBORO
Ross - Cockburn
22-23 Aug.

PIG POINT

ALEXANDRIA
27 Aug.

Feint

WOOD YARD

WHITE HOUSE
BATTERY
1 Sept.

Ft. WASHINGTON
26 Aug.

NOTTINGHAM
Ross
21 Aug.

INDIAN HEAD BATTERY
6 Sept.

Chesapeake Bay

BENEDICT
Ross - Cockburn
19 Aug.

Patuxent River

Wicomico R.

Blakistone I.

St. Marys R.

Potomac

Kettle Bottoms

River

Rappahannock R.

Point
Lookout

Gordon's
Squadron
17 Aug.

hn Carnes

set and darkness was coming on; consequently there was no possibility, for that day, of getting the troops on shore without much confusion, if not danger.

"All therefore remained quiet for the night, with this exception: that the soldiers were removed from the large ships into such as drew least water; which, running up as high as prudence would permit under convoy of the gun-brigs and sloops-of-war, there cast anchor.

"As soon as the dawn began to appear on the morning of the 19th, there was a general stir throughout the fleet. A gun-brig had already taken her station within 150 yards of a village called St. Benedict's, on the [right] bank of the river, where it was determined that the disembarkation should be effected. Her broadside was turned towards the shore and her guns, loaded with grape and round shot, were pointed at the beach to cover the landing of the boats. Being moored fore and aft with spring-cables, she was altogether as manageable as if she had been under sail.

"The rest of the ships were several miles lower down the stream, some of them being aground at the distance of four leagues from this point; but the boats were quickly hoisted out from every one of them, and the river was covered in a trice with a well-manned and warlike flotilla.

"Disembarkation was conducted with the greatest regularity and dispatch, though the stream ran strong against them and some were obliged to row fourteen or fifteen miles backwards and forwards. So strenuously did the sailors exert themselves that by 3 o'clock in the afternoon the whole army was landed, and occupied a strong position about two miles above the village.

"From what I have stated respecting the gun-brig it will be seen that all things were in readiness to meet and repel opposition should such be offered. Her broadside being pointed directly towards the village, whilst it hindered the enemy from bringing down troops in that direction, gave to our people an opportunity of forming and being able to meet in good order whatever force might be posted to check their advance.

"Had a few pieces of artillery been mounted upon the high ground, afterwards taken possession of by us, some execution might have been done upon the boats as they drew towards the beach; but even that would have been trifling because, unless they had had leisure to heat their shot, no artillery in the open country could have long stood before the fire of even a gun-brig, armed as this was with long 32-pounders.

"Each boatload of soldiers, likewise, drew up the moment they stepped on shore, forming line without regard to companies or battalions; whilst parties were instantly dispatched to reconnoiter, and to take possession of every house, as well as to line every hedge in front of the shore where their comrades were arriving. But these preparations, though no more than common prudence required, were unnecessary since there was not only no opposition to the landing but, apparently, no enemy within many miles of the place.

"So much time was unavoidably expended in establishing the different regiments on the ground allotted to them, in bringing up the hospital and commissariat stores, and arranging the materiel that, when all things were ready, the day appeared too far spent to permit an advance into a country the nature and military situation of which we were of course ignorant. The afternoon was accordingly devoted to a proper distribution of the force; which was divided into three brigades, in the following order.

"The first, or light brigade, consisted of the Eighty-fifth, the light infantry companies of the Fourth, Twenty-first and Forty-fourth Regiments, with the party of disciplined Negroes and a company of marines, amounting in all to about 1,100 men; to the command of which Colonel William Thornton of the Eighty-fifth Regiment was appointed.

"The second brigade, composed of the Fourth [King's Own] and Forty-fourth Regiments, which mustered together

1,460 bayonets, was entrusted to the care of Colonel Arthur Brooke of the Forty-fourth.

"The third, made up of the Twenty-first and the battalion of marines and equalling in number the second brigade was commanded by Colonel William Patterson of the Twenty-first.

"The whole of the infantry may therefore be estimated at 4,020 men.

"Besides these, there were landed about 100 artillerymen and an equal number of drivers; but for want of horses to drag them, no more than one 6-pounder and two small 3-pounder guns were brought on shore. Except those belonging to the general and staff officers, there was not a single horse in the whole army. To have taken on shore a large park of artillery would have been, under the circumstances, absolute folly; indeed the pieces which were actually landed proved in the end of very little service, and were drawn by seamen sent from the different ships for the purpose.

"The sailors thus employed may be rated at 100, and those occupied in carrying stores, ammunition, and other necessaries at 100 more. Thus, by adding these together with 50 sappers and miners to the above amount, the whole number of men landed at St. Benedict's may be computed at 4,500.

"This little army was posted upon a height which rises at a distance of two miles from the river. In front was a valley, cultivated for some way and intersected with orchards, at the farther extremity of which the advanced picquets took their ground, pushing forward a chain of sentinels to the very skirts of the forest.

"The right of the position was protected by a farmhouse with its enclosure and out-buildings, and the left rested upon the edge of the hill, or rather mound, which there abruptly ended. On the brow of the hill, and about the center of the line, were placed the cannon, ready loaded and having lighted fuzes beside them. The infantry bivouacked immediately under the ridge, or rather upon the slope of the hill which looked toward the shipping, in order to prevent their disposition from being seen by the enemy should they come down to attack.

"As we were now in a country where we could not calculate upon being safe in rear, any more than in front, the chain of picquets was carried around both flanks and so arranged that no attempt could be made to get between the army and the fleet, without due notice and time given to oppose and prevent it.

"Everything, in short, was arranged with the utmost skill, and every chance of surprise provided against. But the night passed in quiet, nor was an opportunity afforded of evincing the utility of the very soldier-like dispositions which had been made."

Ross's professional troops thus ended their first day on American soil.

2

As CUSTOMARY in the field, the British soldiers took up their arms an hour before daylight on Saturday, 20 August, expecting to move after the sun rose. In what direction, says Lieut. Gleig, none but the general himself appeared to know.

"A rumour indeed prevailed that a flotilla of gunboats upon the Patuxent, commanded by the American Commodore Barney, was the point of attack; and that while the land force advanced up the river to prevent their retreat, armed boats from the fleet were to engage them in front. . . . In this state affairs continued till 4 o'clock in the afternoon when the General suddenly made his appearance in the camp, the bugles sounded, and the regiments formed in order for marching. Nor did many minutes elapse before the word was given, and the army began to move, taking the direction of Nottingham, a town situated on the river, where it was understood that the flotilla lay at anchor."

As Cochrane reported to the Admiralty:

"Ross, with his army, moved towards Nottingham while

our flotilla, consisting of the armed launches, pinnaces, barges, and other boats of the fleet, under command of rear-admiral Cockburn, passed up the river, being instructed to keep upon the right flank of the army for the double purpose of supplying it with provisions and, if necessary, to pass it over to the left bank of the river into Calvert county, which secured a safe retreat to the ships should it be judged necessary."

The same caution and good order that had marked the night's choice of camping ground accompanied the day's march, Lieut. Gleig reports.

"The advanced guard, consisting of three companies of infantry, led the way. These, however, were preceded by a section of twenty men moving before them at the distance of 100 yards; and even these twenty were but the followers of two files sent forward to prevent surprise and to give warning of the approach of the enemy.

"Parallel with the head of the three companies, marched the flank patrols; parties of forty or fifty men which, extending in files from each side of the road, swept the woods and fields to the distance of nearly half a mile.

"After the advanced guard, leaving an interval of 100 or 150 yards, came the light brigade which, as well as the advance, sent out flankers to secure itself against ambuscades. Next to it, again, marched the second brigade, moving steadily on, leaving the skirmishing and reconnoitering to those in front. Then came the artillery . . . and last of all came the third brigade, leaving a detachment at the same distance from the rear of the column as the advanced guard was from its front."

In moving through enemy territory, the British army governed its daily marches by the nature of the terrain over which it passed. If, after only 8 or 10 miles, it came on a piece of naturally well-defended ground, it bivouacked. It did not imprudently push on because the men had not yet reached the point of fatigue. If, however, the troops had marched upwards of 25 miles without coming on a defensible site, only the prospect of losing a large proportion of weary men would halt them before they reached more tenable ground. As Lieut. Gleig reports:

"Our march today was, upon this principle, extremely short, the troops halting when they had arrived at a rising ground distant not more than six miles from the point whence they set out. Having stationed the picquets, planted the sentinels, and made such other arrangements as the case required, fires were lighted and the men were suffered to lie down.

"It may seem strange, but it is nevertheless true, that during this short march of six miles a greater number of soldiers dropped out of the ranks and fell behind from fatigue than I recollect to have seen in any march in the Peninsula of thrice its duration. The fact is that the men, from having been so long cooped up in ships and unused to carry their baggage and arms, were become relaxed and enervated to a degree altogether unnatural. This, added to the excessive sultriness of the day, which exceeded anything we had yet experienced, quite overpowered them.

"The load which they carried likewise was far from trifling. [Probably thirty pounds at least.] Independent of their arms and sixty rounds of ball cartridge, each man bore upon his back a knapsack containing shirts, shoes, stockings, etc., a blanket, a haversack with provisions for three days, and a canteen or wooden keg filled with water."

They found their campsite before sundown—a gentle eminence fronted by open and cultivated country and crowned with several houses surrounded by barns and walled gardens. Though neither flank rested on any particularly well-defended point, the troops could convert almost any one of the houses into a redoubt by extending or condensing their line.

Outposts that stretched completely round the encampment enclosed the entire army within a connected chain of sentinels. No American made an appearance, however, even to reconnoiter.

"Yet," reports Lieut. Gleig, "it cannot be said that the night passed in uninterrupted quiet, for the troops had scarcely lain down when they were disturbed by a tremendous storm of thunder and lightning, accompanied by a heavy fall of rain. The effect of the lightning as it glanced for a moment upon the bivouac, displaying the firelocks piled in regular order and the men stretched like so many corpses beside them, was extremely fine.

"The effect of the rain was not so agreeable for, being perfectly destitute of shelter, we were speedily wet to the skin; and the remainder of our resting time was rendered thereby the reverse of comfortable. But the feeling of fretfulness natural on such an occasion lasted no longer than till the day dawned and the line of march was again formed; when, their former good humour returning, and seasoned in some degree by the fatigues of yesterday, the troops moved on in excellent order and in the highest spirits."

The march on Sunday, 21 August, carried them beyond cultivated cornfields into woods that they called "forests of immeasurable extent." And some of the local guides whom Ross had impressed into his service told the troops that American riflemen lay in ambush. Excitement mounted; commanders strengthened and extended flank patrols, and the advanced guard marched farther ahead—cautiously.

In the course of this day's march, Lieut. Gleig caught a glimpse of American character.

"Having been informed that in a certain part of the forest a company of riflemen had passed the night, I took with me a party of soldiers and proceeded in the direction pointed out, with the hope of surprising them. On reaching the place I found that they had retired, but I thought I could perceive something like the glitter of arms a little farther towards the middle of the wood.

"Sending several files of soldiers in different directions, I contrived to surround the spot. Moving forward, I beheld two men dressed in black coats and armed with bright firelocks and bayonets, sitting under a tree. As soon as they observed me they started up and took to their heels but, being hemmed in on all sides, they quickly perceived that to escape was impossible and accordingly stood still.

"I hastened toward them and, having arrived within a few paces of where they stood, I heard the one say to the other with a look of the most perfect simplicity, 'Stop, John, till the gentlemen pass.'

"There was something so ludicrous in this speech, and in the cast of countenance which accompanied it, that I could not help laughing aloud; nor was my mirth diminished by their attempts to persuade me that they were quiet country people come out for no other purpose than to shoot squirrels.

"When I desired to know whether they carried bayonets to charge the squirrels as well as muskets to shoot them, they were rather at loss for a reply. They grumbled exceedingly when they found themselves prisoners and conducted as such to the column."

The troops approached Nottingham toward the end of the day. They had captured a few stragglers, but the morning's rumors had brought no skirmishing and the men had begun to let down when a smart firing broke out in the woods on their right.

The column closed its order, ready to wheel into line. But the American riflemen who had fired on the British flank patrol vanished among the trees, and the troops—which had continued to move on during the skirmish—marched into Nottingham unopposed.

As Lieut. Gleig noted:

"We found this place (a town or large village capable of containing 1,000 to 1,500 inhabitants) completely deserted. Not an individual was to be seen in the streets or remained in the houses; whilst the appearance of the furniture, etc., in some places the very bread left in the ovens, showed that it had been evacuated in great haste immediately before our arrival."

On the banks of the Patuxent, the town of Nottingham consisted of four short streets, two running parallel with the river and two others crossing these at right angles. Its houses reminded the British of their cottages at home. The substantial farmhouses around the village impressed them.

So did the abundant tobacco fields that stretched for several miles in every direction. Besides the growing and unripe crop, they found barns filled with the previous year's harvest—the whole of which was "of course" seized in the name of His Majesty King George the Third.

"But in the main object of our pursuit we were disappointed," Lieut. Gleig recounts. "The flotilla, which had been stationed opposite to Nottingham, retired, on our approach, higher up the stream. And we were, consequently, in the situation of a huntsman who sees his hounds at fault and has every reason to apprehend that his game will escape."

3

ACCORDING TO Lieut. Gleig, Ross hesitated between returning his troops to Benedict or following the American gunboats. At last, at 8 A.M. Monday, 22 August, he set his column forward in the direction of Upper Marlboro, some ten miles beyond Nottingham.

The troops marched on a road cut through sandy soil, "but in general hard, dusty and, to use an expressive phrase, having a sound bottom. Running as it did for the most part through the heart of thick forests it was also well sheltered from the rays of the sun, a circumstance which, in a climate like this, is of no slight importance."

In the valley village of Marlboro the British army made itself comfortable after having marched upwards of 40 miles, as the roads wound, in three days. Soldiers put together shelters and beds of green corn, which they cut down freely, made off with sheep, and regaled themselves from "orchards and gardens abounding in peaches and other fruits of the most delicious flavour." Officers dined and lodged at the homes of

Marlboro's leading citizens. Ross stayed with Dr. William Beanes.

The marching invaders thus far had done little reconnoitering and obtained scant information. To remedy this evil, Lieut. Gleig reports, "orders had been issued to catch and bring in all the horses that were found in the fields or stables. These orders being punctually obeyed, there were now fifty or sixty in the camp."

With improvised bridles and often with blankets folded for saddles, Ross mounted his artillerymen and improved his reconnaissance with mounted scouts on a sorry variety of horses.

En route to Marlboro that Monday the troops had heard several heavy explosions. So had Cockburn who, in the evening two days earlier, had set out to find and attack the United States flotilla under Com. Barney.

Cockburn led three divisions of some forty armed boats and tenders which carried the marines under Major John Robyns and the marine artillery under Captain James H. Harrison. Captain John Wainwright of *Tonnant* had over-all command, with Captains Thomas B. Sullivan and William S. Badcock leading the first division, Captains Rowland Money and James Somervell leading the second, and Captain Robert Ramsay leading the third.

Leaving their ships at Benedict, Cockburn's armada pulled up the tortuous Patuxent "like stalking through a wood." They kept abreast of Ross's troops to Nottingham where the general struck inland to Upper Marlboro. Joined by overtaking boats from frigate *Severn* with Capt. Nourse and from frigate *Hebrus* with Captain Edmund Palmer, the fleet opened the reach above Pig Point on the river's east bank 22 August.

Here, Cockburn saw Barney's broad pennant. Behind the sloop that flew it, sixteen gunboats strung out in a line; behind these, thirteen tobacco schooners huddled.

And, before Cockburn's eyes, the flagship blew up—followed by fifteen of the gunboats.

Barney earlier had removed their cannons and departed with 400 of his sailors and marines, leaving a fire party of some 100 under his second lieutenant, Solomon Frazier, to destroy the hulls if and when the British came in sight.

Next morning, Tuesday, 23 August, Cockburn left his marines and two divisions of boats at Pig Point, crossed back to the Patuxent's western shore with the third division, and marched overland to join Ross at Marlboro about 4 miles up the Patuxent's west branch.

Firsthand reports differ on whether staff officers sought Cockburn out and brought him to a conference with Ross. In any event, Ross and Cockburn debated their next move until past noon. Their ostensible invasion objective—the American gunboats—had gone up in flames. They had encountered no resistance on the water or on land. The prospect for a successful attack on Washington loomed bright.

Despite scouts' reports that an American force had collected to oppose the British advance, Ross gave the order to march forward along the more circuitous of two roads toward Washington. The Americans could not know whether the British, on this road, headed for Washington, for the Potomac and their fleet, or for Bladensburg.

To Cochrane—with his fleet captain Edward Codrington, in quarters at the Benedict home of "our friend Andrew King . . . who treats us in good friendly hospitality"—Cockburn sent an aide, Lieutenant James Scott, to report destruction of Barney's fleet and the "intended descent upon the Capital."

Cockburn then had his marines, marine artillery, and seamen join Ross's troops; and he ordered a division of boats up to Marlboro, to hold the town and to maintain communication between the army and the remainder of the flotilla which remained at Pig Point to cover a retreat.

"We quitted Marlboro about two in the afternoon," says Lieut. Gleig, "taking the road to Washington . . . till arriving at a point where two roads meet, the one leading to Washington, the other to Alexandria, a strong body of troops with some artillery were observed upon a slope of a height opposite.

"The capture of Washington was now the avowed object of our invasion but the General, like an experienced officer, was desirous of keeping his enemy in the dark as to his plan of operations. While the advanced guard, therefore, reinforced by two additional companies, marched forward to dislodge the party from the height, the rest of the army wheeled to the left, taking the road which leads not to Washington but to Alexandria.

"These movements were not lost upon the enemy who, observing by the dust in what direction the main body had filed off, immediately began to retreat without waiting for the approach of the detachment sent against them.

"As they ascended the hill, however, they made a show of halting and forming a line. Our men moved steadily on in column, covered by one company in extended order along the front. But the enemy, having merely thrown a few round shot with great precision among the skirmishers, broke once again into marching order and were quickly hid by the rising ground.

"As soon as they had disappeared the advance halted and, having remained for about an hour on a little hill to watch their motions, turned to the left and followed the rest of the army, which they found advantageously posted at a place called Wood Yard."

That night, says Lieut. Gleig, "was not spent in as much quietness as usual," an understatement of the nth magnitude.

For, while the soldiers camped a day's march from America's capital, they saw flames burn Stoddert's (or Anacostia) bridge at Washington, the upper of the city's two across the Eastern Branch below Bladensburg ford.

And Lieut. Scott arrived at Cockburn's quarters on the "Melwood" estate of Ignatius Digges at 2 A.M. Wednesday, 24

August, with instructions from Cochrane in Benedict. The invasion commander-in-chief ordered Ross and Cockburn to forget their descent on Washington and return to the fleet.

Upon receiving Cockburn's report of intent to march on Washington, Cochrane had huddled with Capt. Codrington, apparently filled with qualms over risking, with limited forces, an attempt on the capital which might jeopardize the expedition's later objective—New Orleans.

Cochrane sent Lieut. Scott racing back to Cockburn with a message and with instructions to memorize the message's contents and "devour" its paper if captured. Lieut. Scott reported, from Cochrane:

> —That under all circumstances the Rear Admiral [Cockburn] had already effected more than England could have expected with the force under his orders.
> —That he was on no account to proceed one mile farther.
> —Upon receipt of the order, the army was immediately to return to Benedict to re-embark.

When Cockburn relayed the news to Ross, the general declared they could do nothing else but turn back. The admiral insisted they had gone too far to retreat.

"If we proceed, I'll pledge everything that is dear to me as an officer that we will succeed," Cockburn told Ross, according to Lieut. Scott. "If we return without striking a blow it will be worse than a defeat. It will bring a stain upon our arms.

"I know their force," he insisted with his usual arrogance. "The militia, however great their force, will not, cannot, stand against your disciplined troops. It is too late; we ought not to have advanced—there is no choice left us. We must go on."

Lieut. Scott describes Ross as apparently much excited. Striking his hand against his forehead, the general threw caution to the wind:

"Well, be it so!" he exclaimed. "We will proceed."

Ross had independent command of his troops, cooperating with but not subordinate to Cochrane; his decision lay with himself. Cockburn, however, commanded under Cochrane; his decision constituted disobedience of orders.

The fateful determination to push on held for both men intimations of fame and fortune. For while America's capital presented no strictly military object (the comparatively empty Navy Yard offering little in men or stores), Ross and Cockburn could expect, as Cockburn put it, "no small *éclat* to our arms abroad; and to ourselves a more solid gratification if the government, to save the city, be disposed to make a liberal donation of their money."

Booty!

With rockets, Cockburn signaled Capt. Gordon and the Potomac fleet, off Point Maryland, four days away from Fort Washington.

The troops learned of the decision three hours after Lieut. Scott had brought Cochrane's explicit orders to march back to Benedict—when Ross and Cockburn, in the dark of 5 A.M., feinted their forces along the road toward Washington's Eastern Branch bridge. About 4 miles from their night's camp, the troops retraced their steps and headed for Bladensburg.

That Wednesday morning of 24 August, says Lieut. Gleig, started out both cool and agreeable.

"The road, if road it could be called, wound for the first five miles through the heart of an immense forest . . . completely overshadowed by projecting branches of trees so closely interwoven as to prevent a single sunbeam from making its way within the arch. . . .

"But no sooner had we begun to emerge from the woods and to enter the opening country than an overpowering change was perceived. The sun, from which we had been hitherto defended, now beat upon us in full force; and the dust, rising in thick masses from under our feet without a breath of air to disperse it, flew directly into our faces, occasioning the greatest inconvenience both to the eyes and respiration.

"I do not recollect a period of my military life during which I suffered more severely from heat and fatigue."

Men began to fall behind, from absolute inability to keep up. The invasion's emotional strain mounted. Rumors had reached the troops that the Americans had concentrated forces . . . aimed to hazard a battle in defense of the capital.

Bundles of straw, smoking ashes, and scattered orts of campfire meals indicated that considerable bodies of soldiers had spent the night in the neighborhood. And imprints in the road of many feet and hooves indicated close proximity of American troops. With Washington not more than 10 or 12 miles distant, all signs tended to assure the British that "we should at least see an American army before dark."

From being extremely close, the country had opened on every side, with thick groves frequently separating one field from another. From behind these groves cavalry could swoop down on the British column without warning. In one or two places the invaders saw whole rows of paling pulled up from the side of the road to leave open spaces through which several squadrons of horse might gallop.

"Every man held his breath in expectation and prepared himself to form a square in a moment," Lieut. Gleig confesses, and here the so-called Cossacks became peculiarly useful. "They were divided into small parties of six or eight and sent out in different directions to reconnoiter, two of them generally taking post at every suspicious corner, that one might give notice to the column whilst the other watched the motions of an enemy.

"It so happened that these precautions were unnecessary, for whatever might be the strength of the Americans in cavalry, their general did not think fit to employ it in harassing our march. But the very knowledge that every danger was provided against, and that they could not be attacked without having time to make ready, gave the soldiers a degree of steady confidence which they would otherwise have wanted; and the want of which, had the case been different, might have been productive of disorder at a moment when good order was of vital importance."

At this point, the British had marched about 9 miles, during the last four of which the broiling sun and the choking clouds of dust had made marching increasingly arduous. Lieut. Gleig bluntly states:

"If we pushed on much farther without resting, the chances were that at least one half of the army would be left behind."

To prevent this and to give time for stragglers to catch up with the column, commanders ordered a halt on a piece of well-wooded ground watered by a stream which crossed the road.

"Perhaps no halt ever arrived more seasonably than this, or bid fair to be productive of more beneficial effect. Yet," Lieut. Gleig reveals, "so oppressive was the heat that we had not resumed our march above an hour when the banks by the wayside were again covered with stragglers, some of the finest and stoutest men in the army being literally unable to go on."

As noon approached, a heavy dust cloud 2 or 3 miles distant attracted the invaders' attention.

"From whence it originated," Lieut. Gleig declares, "there was little difficulty in guessing, nor did many minutes expire before surmise was changed into certainty.

"For, on turning a sudden angle in the road and passing a small plantation which obstructed the vision toward the left, the British and American armies became visible to one another."

4

WHEN JAMES MONROE went into action on the capital's receipt of British invasion news, he took the field as America's first Cabinet officer to serve as army scout.

"Mr. Monroe," observed French Ambassador Louis Serurier, who had a keen insight into the character of America's current leaders, "is not a brilliant man, and no one expects to find a great captain in him. But he served through the War of Independence with much bravery under the orders and by the side of Washington. He is a man of great good sense, of the most austere honor, the purest patriotism and the most universally admitted integrity. He is loved and respected by all parties."

Before that Thursday of 18 August, Monroe had served (after the President dropped blustery Revolutionary surgeon William Eustis 31 December 1812), as Madison's interim War Secretary, resigning in the hope of becoming commander of the United States Army in the field. When Madison gave the post to Gen. Armstrong, Monroe cautioned the President against allowing a single man to combine the duties of department head and field commander—which Gen. Armstrong proceeded to do.

Monroe saw Gen. Armstrong, like Napoleon, plotting a path to his country's highest office through its battlefields. Now, when Gen. Armstrong insisted that British invaders at the Patuxent's mouth aimed for Baltimore, not Washington, Monroe moved to countervail this blindness.

From Gen. Winder, Monroe obtained Captain Thornton's troop of Alexandria cavalry and, on Friday morning, 19 August, rode toward Benedict. In the saddle as Colonel James Monroe, Madison's zealous Secretary of State for three days scoured the Patuxent and the Potomac neighborhoods, reporting back to the President.

He found farmers moving their Negroes and stock to safety in the interior and, from a pine forest vantage point, watched the British set up camp at Benedict. He reported Cockburn's upriver advance toward Barney's flotilla, and Ross's march toward Nottingham.

On Sunday, 21 August, he left Nottingham as the invaders entered, inferring "that the enemy had moved up the river either against Com. Barney's flotilla at Nottingham, confining their views to that object, or taking that in their way & aiming at the city [Washington] in combination with the force on the Powtowmac. . . ."

From the Washington Navy Yard, Navy Secretary Jones already had advised sending Barney's boats up "to Queen Anne's, with as few men as possible, and a trusty officer to remain there and, in the event of the enemy advancing upon the flotilla in force, to destroy the whole effectually, and proceed to this place." The commodore, accordingly, had taken 400 of his 500 seamen with their guns and ammunition ashore at Pig Point, leaving enough men on each boat to blow the fleet up before rejoining him.

Cockburn saw the fleet burn Monday 22 August.

With arrival of news that the British had entered the Patuxent, Gen. Winder had had his hands full. To pull an army together, he sent proclamations through Maryland, Virginia, and Pennsylvania calling on their militia. For troops arriving through Washington, he set up a rendezvous at Wood Yard encampment, 12 miles in advance of the city; militiamen from the north had orders to rally at Bladensburg under Brigadier-General Tobias E. Stansbury of Baltimore.

Thursday and Friday, 18 and 19 August, held every kind of confusion. While Winder dispatched his expresses outbound, inbound officers passed themselves and their problems through his office. After he had obtained needed scouting support for Monroe, Colonel Allen McLane, cavalry captain in the Revolution, came along with an offer also to reconnoiter the enemy. For McLane, Winder ordered the quartermaster to furnish a horse—and 300 axes with which to fell trees to obstruct the British invasion march.

On the night of 19 August Winder reviewed the Columbia militia on Greenleaf Point where the men, disapproving their odds and ends of arms, demanded rifles. Since Winder had none to issue, he sent the miltiamen home to gather what arms they could and patriotically exhorted in his orders:

"Let no man allow his private opinions, his prejudices or caprices in favor of this or that particular arm or weapon of annoyance be pretended excuse for deserting his post, but seize on those which can be furnished him; or he can command himself resolutely to encounter the enemy and prove that the bravery of freemen fighting for their families, their liberties, can render every weapon formidable."

Next day, Saturday 20 August, Lieutenant-Colonel Frisby Tilghman appeared with 300 Maryland cavalry in blue coats laced with gold, long white pants, stovepipe-style round leather helmets with visor, fur crest and plume, and curved sabers—trumpeters in reverse jacket colors. Winder sent them to Wood Yard to annoy, harass, and impede the enemy march by every possible means, to remove or destroy forage and provisions from before the enemy, and to gain intelligence. Captain Caldwell's troop of city cavalry he sent toward Benedict by way of Piscataway for the same purpose, should the enemy move in that direction.

At noon Gen. Smith brought up the Columbian Brigade of Washington and Georgetown militia with Major George Peter and Captain Benjamin Burch, a soldier of the Revolution; Captains John Doughty and J. I. Stull commanded companies of riflemen—about 1,000—and twelve 6-pounders. Winder sent them toward Wood Yard, and Gen. Stuart took another division of some 1,500, of all arms, across the Eastern Branch.

That night, Winder called all general officers to council at his quarters, Mackgowan's tavern on Pennsylvania Avenue (where British Commissioner for Prisoners Thomas Barclay and his family dined upstairs).

Next day, Sunday 21 August, Winder took command at Wood Yard. Here Barney and 400 flotillamen joined him, and Capt. Miller and 103 marines with three 12-pounders and two 18-pounders on mobile mounts joined Barney.

At this point Winder's combined militia, army, and navy forces of some 3,200 stood on the flank of Ross's column moving to Marlboro. But the quartermaster had not sent Col.

McLane the 300 axes for felling obstructive trees, and Winder, worn out by detail, saw in the situation no way to impede the British advance. Uncertain whether the British would strike at Washington, Fort Washington, or Annapolis, Winder held back from engaging the enemy.

He fell back next day, Monday 22 August, to the Long Old Fields, 8 miles from Washington. This strategic position covered a direct British advance on Washington and both flank approaches—Bladensburg road on the left and the road to Fort Washington on the right.

Having joined Winder and evaluated conditions for himself, Monroe warned Madison at the President's House that he "had better remove the records" and have "materials prepared to destroy the bridges" to the capital. The scene mirrored both military and civilian pandemonium.

Scouting the region, Col. McLane reported to Winder:

". . . the enemy advancing from Nottingham in two columns on the road leading to Upper Marlboro, and on the water in open boats . . . the people not disposed to fight . . . very common to see a white cloth stuck on a pole at a house, a signal of submission . . . roads crowded with men in arms running from the enemy to secure their property, none disposed to fight or obstruct the roads, all panic-struck. . . ."

All day the stage and private carriages passed between Marlboro and Washington without interruption and, on the line of the enemy's encampment, groups of horsemen rode in plain clothes—no doubt, said McLane, spies and guides.

On entering the American camp that night with two militia dragoons, McLane found it "much exposed and as open as a race ground; fires before the tents; and as I approached the house the General had quarters in, rather in the rear of the camp, a number of muskets were discharged from the bullock-guard at a drove of cattle the Commissary had driven into camp in the night. My conclusion was, if General Ross does not rout us this night it will not be our fault, and we shall be no better organized tomorrow."

About midnight Navy Secretary Jones came into camp to join Barney.

An hour later Attorney General Richard Rush informed Winder that President Madison had arrived at a nearby farmhouse. Devoted to James Madison, Rush had served as Comptroller from 1811 until February 1814 when he had succeeded William Pinkney as Attorney General. A thirty-four-year-old Philadelphia lawyer remarkable for "candor without offense," he had favored the war with England from the beginning.

Having written the French Ambassador earlier in the day that hope of saving Washington depended on an engagement at Bladensburg, Col. Monroe stayed in the saddle all night.

At 6 A.M. next morning, Tuesday 23 August, Winder waited on Madison and, at 9 A.M., paraded the militia and Barney's seamen for the President's review.

At noon Maj. Peter's flying artillery ran into British light troops halted at Marlboro, and came back to camp.

The President returned to Washington.

When Winder then left camp, confusion mounted. Rumor took over. Word first spread that the general had gone to Bladensburg to see Gen. Stansbury and the Maryland militia (true), then that he had fallen into the hands of the British (false). At this, District militiamen started a movement to elect their Gen. Smith to Winder's command.

Further compounding the confusion, Monroe and Rush—having news that Ross had moved out of Marlboro to form a junction with Cockburn—rode off to Bladensburg to advise Gen. Stansbury on getting to the British rear, breaking it up, and capturing Cockburn's boats.

Halfway to Bladensburg, Winder learned of Maj. Peter's skirmish with the British light troops and returned to his disturbed encampment at 5 P.M.—with a clear view of the overall situation, but still perplexed as to whether Ross and Cockburn, when they moved, would aim for Washington or Fort Washington.

Deciding on the capital as the probable British objective, until sundown Winder covered the fork in the Old Fields road. One arm led direct to Washington, crossing the Eastern Branch on the bridge near its mouth, broadest and deepest point; the other arm passed over the river at Bladensburg where the British could ford.

On second thought, however—fearing a night attack in which he would lose his artillery superiority and subject his inexperienced troops "to certain, infallible, and irremediable disorder, and probably destruction," and counting on Gen. Stansbury's militia to hold Bladensburg—Winder gave up the fork, ordering his army to retire to Washington on the direct road.

Footsore and fatigued from upwards of four days' marching, dispirited by meager rations and bewildering rumors, Winder's weary troops made what became "literally a run of eight miles" to the capital. Crossing the Eastern Branch bridge into the city, they camped that cold, raw night near the bridge. Many went home for rest, food, and a change of clothing.

Unhampered, Ross and Cockburn moved on Bladensburg.

5

ALONG WITH A Secretary of War who believed the enemy would not attack Washington, along with a quartermaster who could not supply axes for felling trees to impede an enemy advancing through woods, along with local militia poorly uniformed and armed, Winder had the vagaries of distant militia —both the drafted and the volunteer—to cope with as the British army moved toward the capital.

Among the few troops answering his call to the states in the Tenth Military District marched a regiment from Baltimore, epitomizing everything both patriotic and ineffectual that citizen soldiers had embodied in the national defense since 1775.

After less than a year's fighting in the Revolution, Gen. Washington wrote John Reed about militia equipped with a full supply of patriotism but, as soldiers, untrained and inexperienced.

"To be plain," he stated, "these people are not to be depended upon if exposed . . . I suppose it to be the case with all raw and undisciplined troops."

Later he said:

"Had we formed a permanent army in the beginning which, by the continuance of the same men in service, had been capable of discipline . . . we should not have been, the greater part of the war, inferior to the enemy, indebted for our safety to their inactivity, enduring frequently the mortification of seeing inviting opportunities to ruin them pass unimproved for want of a force which the country was completely able to afford, and of seeing the country ravaged, our towns burnt, the inhabitants plundered, abused, murdered with impunity from the same cause."

According to John S. Williams, brigade major and inspector of the Columbian Brigade, "the militia troops under Gen. Winder were mostly without any training or discipline whatever—men drafted from peaceable walks of life, in a peaceable section of the country, habituated to comforts and conveniences, to regular hours and good living, instead of being inured to danger or privation. They were unaccustomed to subordination, and disposed to treat their commanding officers as associates and equals.

"Whatever their capacities might have been, there was no time to draw them out; and whatever the qualifications of their officers they were, with but exceptions, wholly unknown to the commanding general who was therefore unable to designate, for the performance of any particular duty, those who might have been capable of performing it. He could not be sure that any order would be promptly executed or any duty properly performed. To attempt strategic movements with such troops or with a 'multitude of commanders' no better skilled in military matters than their men . . . was a waste of time at least, and time in war is a jewel of inestimable value.

"Experience, in our own and other countries, seems to have demonstrated that the only reliable mode of fighting such troops is behind defensive works or in strong natural positions, where they will not be required to execute maneuvers, and will have as little as possible to apprehend from maneuvers of the enemy."

Like regular troops, militia troops might bear the titles of light infantry, dragoons, artillery, riflemen, etc. but, Maj. Williams points out, "as a cowl does not make a monk, to dress and equip a body of men as light infantry or dragoons does not make them what they are called. They must be disciplined, and have some experience in the peculiar duties, before they are entitled to the name.

"A company of cavalry, formed in the heart of a large commercial city, might choose to assume the name of 'Cossacks' and provide themselves with lances and other suitable equipments, but they would remain, in reality, just what they were before—a parcel of inoffensive clerks or journeymen mechanics."

To shape such militiamen, though individually activated by highest motives, into efficient soldiers required training them to rely on their officers and one another, hardly the work of a day. Lack of such reliance made it practically impossible, in the open field, for even the bravest of patriots to stand against an army of veteran soldiers long disciplined as a single mind in carrying out military tactics.

Lighthearted, thrilled, eager to meet the British, militiamen in uniforms bright with reds and blues shouldered arms and stepped out on roads that led from Virginia and Maryland to the capital of their country. Eighteen-year-old John Pendleton Kennedy, volunteer private from Baltimore, captures the spirit of this American pilgrimage as Lieut. Gleig caught the enemy's invasion advance.

"We marched on Sunday, August 21—our regiment, the Fifth—accompanied by a battalion of riflemen commanded by Major William Pinkney, then recently returned from England where he had been our minister for several years and [until February 1814] Attorney General of the United States.

"We had also with us a company of artillery commanded by Richard B. Magruder, another member of the bar, and a small corps of cavalry from the Baltimore Light Dragoons— Harry Thompson's company—the detachment being under the command of Lieutenant Jacob Hollingsworth.

"A portion of [Major Charles] Sterett Ridgley's Hussars were also in the detachment. These were all volunteers of the city. My father was a member of Hollingsworth's command and, with John Brown, an old schoolmate of mine, and three or four privates of the corps, served as videttes (mounted sentinels, stationed in advance of the pickets) to our brigade.

"It was a day of glorious anticipation that Sunday morning when, with all the glitter of a dress parade, we set forth on our march. As we moved through the streets the pavements were crowded with anxious spectators; the windows were filled with women; friends were rushing to the ranks to bid us good-bye—many exhorting us to be of good cheer and do our duty; handkerchiefs were waving from the fair hands at the windows—some few of the softer sex weeping as they waved adieux to husbands and brothers; the populace were cheering and huzzahing at every corner as we hurried along in brisk step to familiar music, with banners fluttering in the wind and bayonets flashing in the sun.

"What a scene it was, and what a proud actor I was in it! I was in the ecstasy of a vision of glory, stuffed with any quantity of romance. This was a real army marching to a real war. The enemy, we knew, was in full career and we had the certainty of meeting him in a few days.

"Unlike our customary parades, our march now had all

the equipments of a campaign. Our wagon-train was on the road; our cartridge-boxes were filled; we had our crowd of camp servants and followers. Officers rode backward and forward along the flanks of the column with a peculiar air of urgent business, as if it required everything to be done in a gallop—the invariable form in which military conceit shows itself in the first movements towards a campaign. The young officers wish to attract attention, and so seem to be always on the most important messages.

"As for me—not yet nineteen—I was too full of the exultation of the time to think of myself—all my fervor was spent in admiration of this glittering army. I thought of these verses, and they spoke of my delight.

> 'It were worth ten years of peaceful life
> One glance at their array.' "

The Fifth Baltimore Regiment marched on the Washington road under a hot afternoon sky. Reaching Elk Ridge Landing before sundown, they pitched tents on a flat meadow under the hills of the Patapsco's farther bank and formed messes that evening.

Private Kennedy's mess included six tent companions, "gentlemen of good condition," to all of whom the camping experience proved both new and amusing. Accustomed to luxurious living, they treated the "pleasant absurdity" of a supper of fat pork and hard biscuit as a matter to laugh over. They had their own stores in an accompanying wagon, and from the crowd of stragglers who followed the column they took a short, active Negro named Elijah (and called Lige) into mess service.

"The first care after getting our tent up," Private Kennedy relates, "was to hold a consultation about our domestic affairs, and it was then resolved that two of us should in turn serve as housekeeper, successively from week to week. The choice today fell on Ned Schroeder and myself. We were to attend at the giving out of the rations, then to cook them. The mess was not likely to grow fat under our administration."

From the quartermaster the pair obtained a new camp-kettle, five or six pounds of pork, and some hard biscuit. After a two-man conference on how to cook pork, they decided to put the meat into the kettle, fill the pot to the brim with water, and set it over a brisk fire for two hours.

"To make the fire," Private Kennedy confesses, "we resolved to signalize our service by that soldierly act which is looked upon as a prescriptive right—the robbing of the nearest fence of as many rails as suited our purpose."

Which they did like veterans, telling themselves that some time or other, perhaps, Congress would pay for the damage. With the kettle resting on stones in a magnificent blaze, the mess cooks sauntered off to watch evening parade. An hour later they lounged back to look at their kettle—buried in a little mound of hot coals, water all boiled out, and red hot.

In the bottom of this lurid pot Privates Kennedy and Schroeder discovered "a black mess which seemed to be reduced to a stratum of something resembling a compound of black soap in a semiliquid state. And on drawing the kettle out of the fire, and cooling it as quickly as we could by setting it in water, we came to the perception that our supper, or at least as much of it as we had cooked, was a compost of charred bones and a deposit of black fat, the whole plated over with the scales of iron which the heat had brought off in flakes from the kettle.

"Our comrades of the mess gathered around this ruin with amused interest, and we were voted a diploma for our admirable experiment in the art of dressing pork."

Later, with the help of Elijah and their supply wagon, they dined on ham, bread, coffee, and chocolate.

Trusting to a greatcoat which he thought adequate for a summer campaign, John Pendleton Kennedy had left Baltimore without a blanket, and the night came on chilly. Luckily his father rode by the tent, discovered his uncomfortable son, and procured a blanket from a friend in the neighborhood.

"At the regulation hour," reports the young militiaman, "the members of the mess who were not detailed for guard duty—some four of us—crept into our tent and, arranging our blankets into a soft bed, laid down and fell into a hearty sleep which was only broken by the reveille the next morning.

"This was my first night of a regular campaign."

6

"THE NEXT DAY," Private Kennedy continues, "we marched from the Landing to Vansville, about twenty miles—halting an hour or so at Waterloo, then McCoy's Tavern, where we got our dinner—I mean my comrades and myself, having no need and not very willing to try another experiment in cooking for ourselves."

The heat of Monday 22 August, with portions of the road in deep sand, made marching a great trial in the military attire of that day and under the load the soldiers shouldered.

As young Kennedy wrote, "We were in winter cloth uniform, with a most absurd helmet of thick jacked leather and covered with plumes. We carried, besides, a knapsack in which—in my own case—I had packed the greatcoat, my newly acquired blanket, two or three shirts, stockings, etc.

"Among these articles I had also put a pair of pumps which I had provided with the idea that, after we had beaten the British army and saved Washington, Mr. Madison would very likely invite us to a ball at the President's House, and I wanted to be ready for it."

He estimates that his knapsack weighed ten pounds, his Harpers Ferry musket fourteen.

"Take our burden altogether and we could not have been tramping over those sandy roads, under the broiling sun of August, with less than thirty pounds of weight upon us. But we bore it splendidly, toiling and sweating in a dense cloud of dust, drinking the muddy water of the little brooks which our passage over them disturbed, and taking all the discomforts of this rough experience with a cheerful heart and a stout resolve.

"We joked with our afflictions, laughed at each other, and sang in the worst of tune."

He looked on the United Volunteers as the finest company in the regiment—about one hundred strong when in full array, but now counting eighty effective men. The elite company included William Gilmore, merchant of high standing, and Jonathan Meredith, distinguished lawyer; several possessed large fortunes. Young Kennedy rated his comrades highly as soldiers though they represented a class of men not generally expected to endure fatigue.

"There was no body of men in all the troops of Baltimore who were more ready for all service, more persistent in meeting and accomplishing the severest duty. To me, personally, labor and fatigue were nothing. I was inured to both by self-discipline, and I had come to a philosophic conviction that both were essential to all enjoyments of life." He adds: "Besides this bit of philosophy, I was lured by the romance of our enterprise into an oblivion of its hardships."

Leaving Vansville—a one-house town on the top of a hill where the stage changed horses en route to Washington—at dawn Tuesday 23 August, the Volunteers marched slowly, with frequent halts, to Bladensburg which they reached about 5 P.M. Reports of the enemy's movements arrived with the speed of hearsay . . . the British had passed Marlboro, marching on Washington . . . they had taken the direct road to the capital . . . they would come via Bladensburg.

The Fifth Regiment's movements depended to considerable degree on what route the enemy took, and Winder, immediately in front of Ross and retiring slowly before him, sent frequent instructions to Gen. Stansbury.

"Of course we in the ranks knew nothing about these high matters," Private Kennedy notes. "All that we could hear were the flying rumors of the hour, which were stirring enough."

One of Winder's videttes, "a Mr. Floyd, known to us in Baltimore," reached the American troops with a great story to tell. Carrying orders to Gen. Stansbury, he had fallen in with a party of British dragoons from whom he fled for his life. Four of those dragoons chased him over Prince Georges County fields, without side fences to guard them, and every field entered through an old and rickety gate which swung to after his horse with a rapid sweep and a bang that threatened to take off its tail. But having Winder's servant, also mounted on a fleet horse, to open and hold open the gates for him, Mr. Floyd had escaped.

"This was all true as he told it," according to young Kennedy, "except that he was mistaken, as we found out the next day when we joined Winder, in one important particular—and that was that his pursuers were not British dragoons but four members of the Georgetown cavalry who fell into the same mistake. They supposed him a British dragoon, straggling from his corps, and gave him chase, feeling very sure from the direction they had pressed him to take that they must soon drive him into our hands."

In camp near Bladensburg, the United Volunteers pitched tents "on the slope of the hill above the town on the eastern side of the river. Stansbury's brigade of drafted militia were there, and Winder, with the rest of the army which altogether perhaps counted 9,000 men [actually a third of that], was not far off. He was falling back before the march of the enemy, who could not have been more than 10 or 12 miles off.

"The afternoon, towards sunset, was mild and pleasant and we had leisure to refresh ourselves by a bath in the Eastern Branch. Our camp was supplied with every comfort and we did not depend on the United States for our supper, for Lige was sent out to forage—with money to purchase what he wanted."

Lige returned about dark, with a pair of chickens and a handful of tallow candles which, he declared, he had found under the flap of a tent in Gen. Stansbury's brigade. Being sure they had been stolen, he "thought he would restore them to their proper owners."

Private Kennedy had little scruple over keeping the chickens and indulging his tentmates in the luxury of illumination from three or of the candles, each fitted into the band of a bayonet with point stuck into the ground. In such unusual splendor, the group dined on Lige's chickens, ham, and coffee —their table a board—"picked from some neighboring house" —resting on the keg in which they kept their biscuit—Jamison's best crackers.

His feet swollen and sore from the day's march "in boots such as none but a green soldier would ever have put on," Private Kennedy took off his shoes, substituted the neat pair of pumps from the pocket of his knapsack, and enjoyed a cigar as he talked about the next day's battle until the bugler blew taps for the bivouac.

"I was too much excited by the novelty and attraction of my position and by the talk of my comrades in the tent to get asleep much before midnight," he relates. "About an hour after this—one o'clock—we were aroused by the scattered shots of our pickets, some four or five in succession in the direction of the Marlboro road, and by the rapid beating of the long roll from every drum in the camp. Everyone believed that the enemy was upon us, and there was consequently an immense bustle in getting ready to meet him.

"We struck a light to be able to find our coats, accoutrements, etc., but in a moment it was stolen away by some neighbor who came to borrow it only for a moment to light his own candle and, in the confusion, forgot to return it. This gave rise to some ludicrous distresses. Some got the wrong boots, others a coat that didn't fit, some could not find their cross-belts. There was no time allowed to rectify these mistakes.

"I, luckily, was all right, except that I sallied out in my pumps."

After marching upwards of a mile toward what they expected to be the fighting front, Private Kennedy's company received orders to return to camp—and never learned why. On the march back, the sky over Washington reddened; it became "more lurid every moment, and at last we could discern the flames."

As the Baltimore militiamen lay down again to sleep, a dispatch arrived with information that Winder held the Eastern Branch bridge and had burned Stoddert's bridge to impede the enemy's march. In consequence, the British must march on the Bladensburg road. Gen. Stansbury ordered the regiment to break camp.

"Here was new excitement—everything was gathered up in a few moments. All our baggage was tossed into our regimental wagon—knapsacks, provisions, blankets, everything but our arms. Among them went my boots."

Like stagehands shifting scenery, the Baltimore troops struck their tents and packed them away. In half an hour from the time of receiving orders, they took the road in full column of march.

"Descending into the village, we crossed the bridge and moved toward Washington. But after making about two miles at a very slow pace we found ourselves brought to a halt, and after this we loitered, as slow as foot could fall, along the road, manifestly expecting some order that should turn us back towards the village we had left.

"What a march that was! I never was so sleepy in my life."

Like his young companions, Private Kennedy had not felt the fatigue of the day's march because of his exhilaration during the early part of the night. Now, an hour or two before daylight, fatigue returned with double force. He slept as he walked. At every halt, entire platoons lay down in the dusty road and slept until officers gave the word to move on. "The burning bridge lighted the whole southern sky, but it had no power to attract our gaze," he later wrote.

"At length, when we had reached a hill some three miles on our route, we were marched into a stubble field and told we might rest until daylight. Here we threw ourselves upon the ground without any covering, exposed to the heavy dew which moistened the earth and hung upon the stubble, and slept. Mine was the sleep of Endymion. When I awoke I was laying on my back with the hot sun of a summer morning [Wednesday 24 August] beaming upon my face.

"Our orders then were to march back to Bladensburg."

7

PROBABLY no American military leader ever had to cope with a greater variety and complexity of problems, to make more decisions based on insufficient and contradictory information, and to work with so many untried officers and soldiers hurried piecemeal to help him fight a disciplined enemy as did Gen. Winder from 18 through 24 August. Retiring from Old Fields the evening of 23 August, many of his troops only reluctantly obeyed orders to move back to where their commander believed they could best (1) protect the capital, or (2) support Fort Washington, or (3) join Gen. Stansbury to attack the British rear if the enemy marched toward Annapolis and Baltimore.

Winder held his command under the influence of elder supervisors, all of whom went into the field with his army— the President, the Secretary of War, the Secretary of State. Madison, Armstrong, and Monroe showed little individual consistency and no harmony as a group, but their separate intimations, from superior in rank to subordinate, put considerable pressure on Winder.

Though Winder made no attempt to evade responsibility for the campaign, he could not, under the circumstances, provide what his militia troops most needed—confidence in their general. They had no personal knowledge of him; they could only see that the nation's leaders showed distrust of his capacities by keeping him in a constant state of instruction and advisement.

After his army's run from Old Fields to Washington the evening of 23 August, Winder rode at 8 P.M. to inform Madison of the state of things. At the President's House he expected to find the Cabinet heads, but they had gone home. He went to Gen. Armstrong's and conferred.

Returning toward the Eastern Branch bridge, he left his borrowed horse (both of his own already exhausted by the day's riding) at a tavern and walked. In the dark, he fell severely into a ditch and injured his right arm and ankle. He finally limped into camp.

Detaching a party of volunteers to burn Stoddert's bridge, he posted Capt. Burch's artillery at the Eastern Branch bridge and sent a party of regular infantry half a mile beyond it to prevent surprise. From Commodore Thomas Tingey, commanding the Navy Yard, he begged powder, boats, and combustibles to make destruction of the bridge sure at any moment. He turned in between 3 and 4 A.M., and "snatched about an hour or two of sleep, rose, and proceeded to gather my attendants and horses, much exhausted and worn down by the incessant action of the three preceding days. . . ."

Gen. Winder took up his burdens on the morning of America's darkest day—24 August 1814—in headquarters near the Navy Yard, at the house of Dr. Andrew Hunter, schoolmaster for midshipmen.

Among other chores, Winder detached a troop of Virginia cavalry to reconnoiter down the Bladensburg road toward the enemy, sent a note to the Navy Secretary urging that Com. Barney occupy the batteries at Greenleaf Point and the Navy Yard in event the British carried out an attack there, and wrote an order on the War Department armorer for the arms and ammunition which Colonel George Minor's Virginia militia could not get the night before from Colonel Henry Carberry, "charged with the business," because the colonel had left town and gone "to his seat in the country."

When Madison arrived at Winder's headquarters for a Cabinet council-of-war with the general, the President found Navy Secretary William Jones already there, concerned with protecting the nearby Yard from British invaders. State Secretary James Monroe, after a long night in the field, arrived soon after, eager to get into action rather than to sit and talk. Richard Rush, youngest of the Cabinet officers, followed. After about an hour came Treasury Secretary George Washington Campbell, United States Senator from Tennessee until the previous February; he had a vigorous mind, but slow, and his initials—GWC—said the Federalists, meant "Government Wants Cash." Eventually, Army Secretary John Armstrong reluctantly filled out the group.

To this meeting, unique in American history, the participants brought many and varied characteristics—but not military perception.

As they saw the problem . . . a British army of 9,000 or 10,000 Wellington veterans (according to flying rumor) marched on Washington against 5,000 raw American militia, salted by some 900 regulars—occasioning, as Secretary Campbell later described, "considerable agitation in the minds of the citizens."

Conversation from then on, reports an attending staff officer, "was rather desultory; first one suggestion was made and commented on, and then another; no idea seemed to be entertained that it was necessary to come instantly to a decision how we should act, and to set immediately about it."

Winder listened.

Gen. Armstrong, never a very agreeable person to hold a discussion with, "his arsenal of arguments consisting in too great part of oaths, sneers, and sardonic smiles," suggested that the enemy might lay a bridge of pontoons if the Eastern Branch bridge were blown up. No one else understood how, without enough horses to transport their artillery and baggage, the British could contrive to carry the pontoons needed to lay a bridge over half a mile of river.

At the close of the meeting, Maj. Williams later revealed, "there was still as much consternation and perplexity as if Ross had that morning dropped suddenly with his army from the clouds, instead of having been, as we are assured, watched at every step of his leisurely progress for four days."

At 10 A.M. intelligence arrived that Ross, after his feint toward Washington along the road to the Eastern Branch bridge, had turned toward Bladensburg. Whereupon the council-of-war fell apart. Monroe offered to join Gen. Stansbury, and left the meeting for Bladensburg. Soon after, Winder followed. Armstrong followed Winder. Jones went to the Navy Yard. Madison and Rush prepared to ride to the battlefield. After seeing his duelling pistols strapped around the President's waist as Madison mounted his horse, Campbell also left; but instead of following the Cabinet members he rode home to Tennessee where, apparently tired of trying to raise money for the war, he wrote out his resignation from office.

On the way to Bladensburg with Rush, Madison observed that Gen. Armstrong might render useful assistance in arrangements for the forthcoming battle.

"It would be best that the requisite sanction to it should be at hand," the nation's commander-in-chief said to explain his presence in the field, "preventing thereby, at a moment so important, any possible embarrassment arising from the claims or duties of the commanding general."

Winder again faced Cabinet supervision. The Secretary of War would issue battle orders and, should the commanding general demur, the President would stand by to straighten matters out!

As Winder hurried toward Bladensburg to meet the British, Col. Minor's eager troops found themselves left behind, desperately trying to get flints for their muskets from a young storekeeper who, after company officers counted

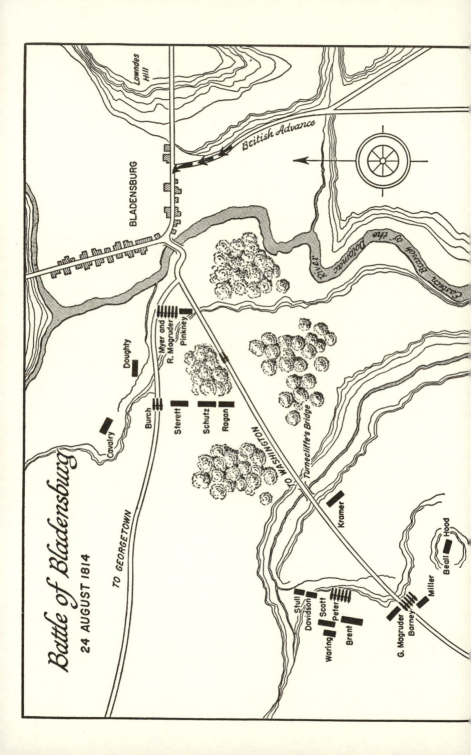

Battle of Bladensburg

24 AUGUST 1814

them out, had to count them over again—and then insisted on the colonel signing receipts. But the foul-ups Winder left behind did not hold a candle to those he rode forward to face.

On the previous day, Gen. Stansbury had not carried out orders to take his Baltimore brigade down the Bladensburg–Marlboro road, pleading the exhaustion of Lieutenant-Colonel Joseph Sterett's Fifth Regiment (young Kennedy's). Instead, Gen. Stansbury had encamped on Lowndes Hill until, at 2:30 A.M., he had a disconcerting express from Winder announcing the retreat from Old Fields to Washington and calling on Gen. Stansbury to resist if the enemy should come to Bladensburg.

Gen. Stansbury had laid the situation before his regimental commanders—Lieutenant-Colonel John Ragan, late captain of U. S. Rifles, Lieutenant-Colonel John H. Schutz, Col. Sterett, and Maj. Pinkney. Feeling that they could not defend the Bladensburg hill with men worn down by hunger and fatigue, the council members decided that they, too, should move into Washington and help defend the capital on the spot.

Gen. Stansbury gave orders to strike tents and, about 3:30 A.M., his brigade passed over the Bladensburg bridge on the road to Washington. Securing his rear from surprise, he then had halted so that his men might cook their provisions and refresh themselves. At daylight he had moved on to the foot of a hill near a brickyard, about 1½ miles out of Bladensburg.

Gen. Stansbury rode to the top of the brickyard hill that 24 August morning, spied out the countryside for Britishers, and rode down the hill again—to receive another express from Winder. Once more Winder called on him to stand and oppose the enemy should Ross come through Bladensburg.

Gen. Stansbury assembled another council-of-war, which again decided to march toward Washington. But, as he ordered up the wagons, further "positive orders" arrived from Winder to give the enemy battle at Bladensburg.

Retracing his steps to an apple orchard half a mile from

where the Bladensburg–Washington road forked to Georgetown, he stationed the regiments of Colonels Ragan and Schutz
behind the orchard.

In front of the orchard—150 yards from the fork and 300
yards from the Bladensburg bridge—Army Engineer Wadsworth earlier had hastily thrown up a barbette battery of
earthwork. Here, Gen. Stansbury posted 150 artillerymen and
six 6-pounders under Captains Joseph Myer and Richard B.
Magruder. To their right he placed Maj. Pinkney's 150 riflemen.

With their 6-pounders, the artillerymen had an effective
range of up to 800 yards; they could disable at 900. With their
rifles, Maj. Pinkney's sharpshooters could hit a foot-square
mark at 250 yards, and kill a horse at 400; but they could fire
only one round per minute, using powder horn and ramrod,
and a rifle had no bayonet. Guns and rifles commanded the
bridge. Col. Sterett's crack Fifth Regiment backed them up.

"Hoping that Gen. Winder would join me before the
battle would commence, and occupy the ground in my rear
as a second line," Gen. Stansbury rested.

Winder reached the Bladensburg bridge close to noon . . .
from Washington, Gen. Smith's District brigade came along
behind . . . from Annapolis, Lieutenant-Colonel William Dent
Beall, officer of the Revolution, and Colonel Thomas Hood
marched over the bridge with 750 militia . . . as the British
column came into sight along the river road.

American troop dispositions changed with the minutes as
Ross's column closed . . . Francis Scott Key, former lieutenant
and quartermaster in Maj. Peter's battery, helped Gen. Smith
examine arrangements proposed for the Washington brigade
. . . Col. Monroe conferred with Gen. Stansbury . . . and
Gen. Stansbury debated relative rank with Gen. Smith.

Past this confusion, Madison and Rush rode down the
turnpike toward Bladensburg in search of Winder. Near the
bridge, a horseman stopped them.

"On approaching the town," Madison records, "we learned from William Simmons that Winder was not there, and that the enemy were entering it."

President and Attorney General had put themselves between the opposing armies! They wasted no time in getting back to Winder.

With the battle about to begin, Madison moved to the rear. Within sight of the front line, the President sat one of Charles Carroll's horses, his own having gone lame. With him sat Cabinet members Rush, Monroe, and Armstrong, Chief Clerk John Graham, Gen. John Mason, commissioner of prisoners, Col. Decius Wadsworth, friend Tench Ringgold; nearby horsemen included Alexander McKim, Baltimore member of Congress, and a number of friends.

"The excitement caused by the invasion," as described by one reporter, "reached the inhabitants of Washington and Georgetown, and many went to the scene of the battle in carriages, on horseback, and on foot. It was something like the coummunity turning out to see a fire."

Which of the military cooks present that morning put what ingredients into the tactical broth does not come clear. The final lines, as the British saw them, do.

When the enemy tramped into sight, Gen. Stansbury's second line had formed in order of battle more than a quarter-mile behind the first line of artillery and riflemen commanding the bridge. And the Fifth Regiment, which Gen. Stansbury originally had stationed where it could support and give confidence to the first line, had backed up the rising ground behind the orchard to fill out the second line's left.

The second line now stretched from the Washington turnpike to the Georgetown road, clearly in the enemy's sight, within reach of his rockets, without cover, so far back that the forward guns and rifles would have the whole British force to contend with.

Some 380 cavalrymen under separate and independent

commanders held a position to the left and somewhat to the rear of this line; the regulars—125 hungry and tired dragoons under Lieutenant-Colonel Jacint Laval, a Frenchman and experienced officer—could hardly sit their horses and their horses could hardly move after days of patrolling.

With the British in view, Winder also brought up beside the second line's left three of Capt. Burch's 6-pounders from the District's brigade.

At the same time, he moved one of Pinkney's rifle companies from right to left of the Baltimore battery in the front line, and further supported the first line's left with 150 District riflemen of Capt. Doughty's company.

Capt. Doughty's riflemen, like those of fellow Capt. Stull's company, carried not rifles but muskets. With their smoothbore muskets whose falling flint in the hammer ignited a pan of powder which set off a muzzle-loaded powder charge, the riflemen could fire one round every fifteen seconds under ideal conditions—using fixed ammunition which combined powder and ball in a single unit. But they could seldom hit a man-sized target at 100 yards. They could, however, fire in destructive volleys without true aiming, at short ranges; and a musket carried a bayonet for close combat.

War Secretary Armstrong had refused to supply rifles, of which the Washington arsenal had plenty from Harpers Ferry forge, telling Capt. Stull they were for the northern army. Capt. Stull's men had gone to Wood Yard with tomahawks. Only on 21 August had they got muskets.

Winder laid out a third line half a mile behind Gen. Stansbury's Baltimore troops. On a ridge that stretched across the turnpike here—where the highway rose up a long hill after dipping into a ravine at Turnecliffe's small bridge—Winder placed Gen. Smith's brigade of Washington and Georgetown militia with their left on the brow of the curving ravine and their right at the turnpike. On the other side of the road, Col. Miller's marine company linked the Washington brigade with the Maryland militia of Colonels Beall and Hood, occupying an eminence on the far right where they looked down on the ravine and the bridge.

That this third line stood defensively ready for Gen. Stansbury's troops to fall back on, Maj. Pinkney in the first line and Col. Sterett in the second did not know.

On the hill behind this third line President Madison, Cabinet members, and entourage sat their horses, along with civilians come to watch the soldiers fight.

Altogether, Winder's force in the field as the British entered Bladensburg totaled about 5,400 by his own official count, of which some 625 comprised regular United States infantry, cavalry, and marine troops. The 4,775 volunteer and standing militia came from Maryland, Virginia, and the District of Columbia.

8

NAMED IN HONOR of Thomas Bladen, early Maryland governor, Bladensburg lay close to the District of Columbia line on the Eastern Branch's left bank, about 5 miles from Congress House. The Baltimore stage stopped daily, en route to Washington, as it entered this village of 1,200 population just after passing Lowndes Hill.

With his advanced party, Britain's General Robert Ross ascended the hill at 12:45 P.M. and, from the second story of Colonel Robert Bowie's residence, thoroughly surveyed the scene and studied his problem.

He saw the turnpike turn left at the river, where stone and brick houses stretched north along its bank. Passing over a wooden bridge some 120 feet long and 12 feet wide, marking the head of river navigation, the road then curved for a short distance north and west along the stream on a sort of causeway bordered by small trees and bushes close to the water.

Ross examined the army Winder had drawn up in the 45-degree triangle formed here by the two rolling roads—straight ahead to Washington, right to Georgetown. The triangle's apex held advanced artillery and riflemen, their guns and rifles trained on the bridge; half a mile past the bridge, the second line stretched across the triangle from the Washington turnpike, behind an orchard, over a field, to the Georgetown road; and, a mile past the bridge, beyond the ravine and the capital's grassy duelling grounds at Turnecliffe's bridge, Ross saw the third, reserve line.

Cockburn thought he looked at an American army of at least 9,000. Ross and he had marched to the battle with about 4,500 only. And in heat which had started at 98 degrees that morning even the scarlet-coated Peninsula veterans and the seasoned marines, seamen gunners, and rocket men reached Bladensburg with parched tongues hanging out—having left many dead of fatigue along the road.

But the British commanders had no misgivings about engaging the Americans at once.

For one thing, Ross had found the town unoccupied and the bridge intact (since Winder held that destruction of any bridge from Benedict to Washington would not stem the invaders for more than ten minutes. Of a different opinion, Gen. Stansbury had ordered forty horsemen with axes to destroy it—and never learned why they failed to carry out his order). Too, in his march with Cockburn—a practically unchallenged frolic—Ross had absorbed some of the marauding admiral's scorn for the American militiaman's military ability. And, third, Cockburn had spelled out for him the disorganized defense that made Washington a tempting plum.

When, therefore, Col. Thornton proposed immediately to move his first brigade of 1,100 men—despite the rigors of their morning's march—on the road to Washington, Ross acceded.

Harry Smith, who called Ross cautious, protested. This slim twenty-seven-year-old captain had met Ross on the retreat to Corunna and become his major of brigade, serving on the present march as Ross's deputy adjutant-general. He had worked closely with seasoned campaigners since 1805 in Spain, Sweden, Portugal. He urged Ross to feint higher upriver, find a vulnerable point of attack, and use the support of the other two brigades when these moved up. To his horror, Ross ordered Col. Thornton's advance at once.

The American artillery already had shown its accuracy with a well-directed carronade which had forced the British to take cover at Lowndes Hill—the very first shot costing them one killed and two wounded.

Posting light companies of the Eighty-fifth behind trees along the river and behind houses and barns in the village, and with rocket tubes on elevations above the trees to serve as artillery, Col. Thornton pushed at double quick time toward the head of the bridge.

From Maj. Pinkney's first line, Baltimore's artillery opened fire as the enemy reached the bridge. Capt. Burch's two Georgetown guns on the turnpike aided with grapeshot.

Lieut. Gleig reports that the first American discharge swept down "almost an entire company . . . the riflemen likewise began to gall us from the wooded bank with a running fire of musketry. And it was not without trampling upon many of their dead and dying comrades that the light brigade established itself on the opposite side of the stream."

With his riflemen, Maj. Pinkney observed the action otherwise. He reports:

"Assisted by some discharges of rockets (which were afterward industriously continued), the enemy made an effort to throw across the bridge a strong body of infantry, but he was driven back at the very commencement of it, with evident loss, by the artillery in the battery, which principally acted upon the street or road near the bridge, and he literally disappeared behind the houses. The effort was not immediately repeated, but the artillery continued to fire, with a view, as it seemed, to interrupt the discharge of rockets, as in some degree it did, and otherwise to check the enemy's operations.

"After a long pause . . . a second attempt was made to

cross the bridge, with increased numbers and greater celerity of movement. This, too, was encountered by the artillery in the battery, but not with its former success."

Inexorably crossing the stream on this second attempt, and wheeling to right and left of the turnpike, the British cleared the thickets of American skirmishers.

"A large column of the enemy," Maj. Pinkney states, "which was every moment reenforced either by way of the bridge or by the ford immediately above it, was able to form on the Washington side and to menace the battery and the inadequate force by which it was to be supported."

The Baltimore artillery, finding it difficult to depress the guns in their breastwork's half-formed embrasures to meet the enemy's near approach, fell back. Capt. Burch abandoned a disabled gun. A musket ball broke Maj. Pinkney's arm. The riflemen, too, fell back.

To the British this looked like an easy victory. Throwing knapsacks and haversacks into squad piles, the light brigade extended ranks and pushed toward the American second line in files of skirmishers 10 paces apart.

But for three hours—until four o'clock that afternoon— the Americans continued to fight the British at Bladensburg, action developing into two separate battles "as distinct as if they had taken place on different days and with different armies."

Winder saw Ross's weakness as the first enemy wave came on. He advanced Gen. Stansbury's three regiments, which checked the British with heavy fire. Moving forward to re- cover the lost ground, they drove the British back to the river thicket, and pinned them there.

But Col. Brooke's Forty-fourth, part of Ross's second brigade, came into Bladensburg, drifted behind houses and barns, and forded the river upstream under its cover of bushes and trees. The Fourth, also Brooke's, marched close behind them, and Ross's rockets began to make themselves felt as

Winder saw the second brigade move up the Georgetown road to encircle Gen. Stansbury's left.

Adapting skyrockets to warfare in 1804, Englishman Congreve had replaced paper bodies with iron and evolved a weapon which, propelled by black powder, had proved useful on both sea and land. The British navy's 32-pound rocket —42 inches long and 4 inches diameter on a 15-foot stabilizing shaft—carried an incendiary, case shot, or explosive warhead. It could be shot from a hollow copper tube supported by a tripod, from a troughlike chamber set on the ground, or from a simple launcher mounted on the cart that carried the rockets.

Notoriously inaccurate in flight, its bark—or screech— proved far more effective than its bite. The British, therefore, used it to demoralize green troops, to panic them with its eerie track and appalling noise.

Ross's first rockets passed over Winder's second line, throwing American cavalry horses and artillery mules into a frenzied stampede. When Cockburn's rocket men flattened their missiles' trajectory, America's militiamen panicked, too.

With Col. Brooke's Forty-fourth encircling the American second line's left flank and Col. Thornton's Eighty-fifth pushing to cover in the orchard on its front, the inexperienced militia broke amid the whining rockets. Despite every effort to rally, Col. Ragan and Col. Schutz found themselves alone with thirty or forty men each—the rest "flying in utmost precipitation and disorder."

Winder raced along the line to Col. Sterett's Fifth Regiment. With the help of Capt. Burch's artillery on the left, these volunteer infantrymen had held their ground when the advanced Baltimore artillery and riflemen had moved back to a position on a rise behind them; and Winder hoped that their fire would scour the British when the enemy came out of the orchard's cover.

But, advancing singly to take annoying positions from which they could shoot at this remainder of Gen. Stansbury's second line without absorbing much damaging fire in return, Col. Thornton's infantry harassed the Fifth.

When Col. Brooke's Forty-fourth fought its way up the Georgetown road to the line's left flank and began to deploy into the field, Winder ordered the Baltimore volunteers to retire up the hill and form with the Baltimore artillery and riflemen.

His order ended the first Bladensburg battle.

For, Winder reported, "this corps which had heretofore acted so firmly, evinced the usual incapacity of raw troops to make orderly movements in the face of the enemy, and their retreat in a very few moments became a flight of absolute and total disorder."

Like most other citizen soldiers in the action, Col. Sterett's crack Fifth knew nothing of the third line waiting for them to fall back on. Through fields and along the Georgetown road, they fled toward Montgomery Court House. They carried everything with them, literally and figuratively, crushing Col. Laval's weary cavalry troop, "horses and all," in the tumult of their flight which began at about two o'clock.

"We made a fine scamper of it," said Private Kennedy, who still wore the dancing pumps he had packed when he left Baltimore to defend the capital. Bearing a companion with a bullet-broken leg, he lost his musket "in the melee." The enemy loomed so formidable that, says another of his companions in the rout, "if we had remained ten minutes longer they would have either killed or taken the whole of us . . . the bullets and grapeshot flew like hailstones about me and I was compelled to make headway for a swamp. . . ."

Despite Winder's pre-Bladensburg zeal, despite his personal valor in the battle, he had not the requisite genius to win with militia against veterans in the open field.

Lieut. Gleig summed up the first Bladensburg battle succinctly:

"Of the personal courage of the Americans there can be no doubt; they are, individually taken, as brave a nation as any in the world. But they are not soldiers; they have not the experience nor the habits of soldiers. It was the height of folly, therefore, to bring them into a situation where nothing but that experience and those habits will avail."

Lieut. Gleig also pointed out:

"When two lines oppose each other, very little depends upon the accuracy with which individuals take aim. It is then that the habit of acting in concert, the confidence which each man feels in his companions, and the rapidity and good order in which different movements can be executed are alone of real service."

This Com. Barney now proved as the second battle of Bladensburg got under way.

9

Joshua Barney started the morning of 24 August outraged. His flotilla blown up, for days past he and his seamen had manhandled and horsed cannons and powder over country roads from Pig Point to Washington without firing a shot. The afternoon before, in order of battle at Old Fields, his sailors and Capt. Miller's marines had waited under the hot sun to meet an enemy that did not appear until, at sunset, Winder had recommended withdrawal of the Navy's heavy guns with the exception of one 12-pounder to cover the retreat to Eastern Branch bridge.

After putting his seamen into the marine barracks for the night, Barney had conferred with Winder at 2 A.M. about guarding the bridge and, next morning, found himself left behind—defending a bridge of no present importance while the soldiers and the Cabinet of the United States raced out of Washington to meet the British at Bladensburg. Angrily Barney sought out the President and Navy Secretary.

Declaring that a midshipman and a dozen sailors could blow up the bridge, he told them—in salty terms reported to have left no doubt about his pent-up feelings and those of his men—that the country needed the Navy's fighting power at Bladensburg.

"A large part of his men were tall, strapping Negroes," reports fifteen-year-old Paul Jennings, body servant born a slave on the President's Montpelier estate. "Mr. Madison asked Com. Barney if his Negroes would not run on the approach of the British. 'No, sir,' said Barney, 'they don't know how to run; they will die by their guns first.'"

Rolling out three 18-pounders—each weighing some 4,200 pounds on an 800-pound ships' carriage—and two 12-pounders, Barney headed his 400 seamen for Bladensburg in an extraordinary procession. Some of the sailors, in shoulder harness, helped the horses pull the big guns; others, shoeless, hit the road armed with muskets and handspikes and cutlasses, full of fight. Behind, mules hauled carts filled with powder, balls, and shells ransacked from the Navy Yard.

The commodore galloped ahead on his big bay, arriving over the District line as the first Bladensburg battle began. Selecting a position in Winder's third line, on the turnpike next to Capt. Miller's marines, commanding the road up from Turnecliffe's bridge and the ravine, Barney sent an officer back to hasten his toiling men—"and they came up on a trot."

In the hour that Winder's inexperienced militia under Gen. Stansbury grappled with Ross's veterans at the Bladensburg bridge, along the orchard, and in the field between the roads to Washington and Georgetown, Barney got his sweating seamen into fighting order.

He planted his two 18-pounders on the highway, his three 12-pounders to their right. All sailors not needed to fight the 18-pounders he stationed behind the 12-pounders, as infantry with the marines. Barney's force constituted the effective center of the American third line.

To the left, Gen. Smith's District brigade covered the wide, shallow ravine for 150 yards to where it ended in a bluff. On the bluff stood Capt. Stull's company of riflemen (with muskets) and Capt. Davidson's company of light infantry. Between them and the Navy guns, Maj. Peter trained his six 6-pounders from an eminence that enabled them to cover part of the second line and Turnecliffe's bridge.

Behind these, across the slope of the hill overlooking the ravine, stretched Major Henry Waring's and Major Samuel Maynard's battalions of Maryland militia, Lieutenant-Colonel William Scott's detachments of Thirty-sixth and Thirty-eighth Regiment regulars, Col. Brent's Second Regiment of District infantry, and Col. George Magruder's First.

About 250 yards on Barney's right, Cols. Beall and Hood held their eminence, an abrupt hill, with the Maryland troops they had brought through Bladensburg only minutes before the British arrived. And in front of Barney, close to where turnpike crossed ravine, Lieutenant-Colonel Kramer's detachment of Maryland militia stood over Turnecliffe's bridge as a delaying force.

With its Army artillery and heavy Navy guns, the American line thus could rake the road, the bridge across the ravine, and the entire top of the curving ravine itself. Barney personally helped his gunners train their pieces.

Waiting, the third line watched the end of the first battle —saw Winder's futile efforts to rally panicked militiamen who knew nothing of this defensive line on which they could have re-formed. The watchers saw British seeping down the Georgetown road to flank Gen. Stansbury's left, saw redcoats skirt the orchard to push through the field, saw a third column make its steady way along the Washington turnpike toward the ravine—all driving the defeated front lines in scattered flight over the face of the Maryland landscape.

Buoyed by victory, Ross's invaders now swung over from the Georgetown road and the open field to combine with the column moving down the turnpike. Outnumbering the Americans two to one, they came in for an attack on the third line's center.

The time: approximately 2 P.M.

The enemy hit Col. Kramer's delaying force first, while

skirmishers covered their flanks in the fields and woods. Col. Kramer slowly fell back, on Col. Beall's right.

The enemy continued, in heavy column, toward Barney's guns. Their rockets erratically whooshed overhead, but failed to demoralize the seamen, who withheld their fire. When Barney ordered a single 18-pounder into action, it completely cleared the road with a single shot, killing ten and sending the British column's rear to cover.

Col. Thornton's first brigade, moving toward the American left, halted in the ravine. And while Col. Thornton got off his horse to cross on foot to look over the situation on the American right, Ross himself (who already had had one horse shot under him) came up to organize the forces which Maj. Peter's 6-pounders now pinned down with a continuous cross-fire.

Twice more, under Ross's guidance, the British advanced to dislodge the stubborn American resistance. Twice again their frontal attack ran into the severest and most precise artillery fire they had "ever in their experience" encountered. From Capt. Miller's marines their close ranks met a withering fire.

Ross waited for a fresh column of the Fourth Regiment to come up before extending his assault through the woods on the American right.

Under Col. Thornton, then, he sent a force into an open field to within 50 yards of Barney's guns. Down on Col. Thornton came the American 12-pounders' canister shot, staggering the regiment and badly wounding Col. Thornton.

Before the British could re-form under Col. Brooke, Capt. Miller went after them with his bayonet-wielding marines and Barney's sailors armed with their cutlasses, handspikes, and muskets, shouting "Board 'em! Board 'em!" Cutting up the attackers, who "declined" to meet bayonet with bayonet, the naval forces drove the enemy back to cover in the wooded ravine, and returned to stations.

A British sharpshooter having put a bullet in the head of

Barney's horse, the commodore took position on foot behind an 18-pounder. At this point he counted fifteen of his 500 men and officers dead, his mules stampeded by rockets which hit and exploded an ammunition box, teamsters of his reserve ammunition wagons run off under cover of the excitement and confusion. Wounded, Capt. Miller also had gone out of action.

On the commodore's left, Maj. Peter's guns had contributed to Barney's three repulses of British frontal attacks on the road through the ravine and had supported Col. Magruder in throwing back redcoats who had sought to flank the battery's left. Now, facing another British attempt to flank him, Maj. Peter saw Col. Scott's regulars and Col. Brent's militia fighting in his support. The situation looked good; with Captains Stull and Davidson helping, together they could disperse and capture the exhausted British—perhaps bring them to surrender in a few minutes.

But now Gen. Winder, after a long and fruitless chase to arrest or direct the flight of his first and second lines, arrived on the third line.

Seeing Maj. Peter with apparent difficulty holding the left, believing Barney could not hold the right, and unwilling to sacrifice lives trying to retrieve a victory, Winder gave orders for Gen. Smith to call for the reserves' retreat.

Unbelieving, many of his men not yet having fired a shot, Gen. Smith moved his District troops back 500 or 600 paces. When Winder gave him a second order, he retired to heights west of the turnpike gate and the Washington city line.

So Barney's seamen and marines found themselves, with little help from the combined Beall-Hood-Kramer group on the right, holding the Washington turnpike alone.

And Ross, who could see how small and unprotected on both flanks his stubborn opposition now stood, sent the British Fourth wide on Barney's right; the Eighty-fifth and portions of the Forty-fourth he sent against Barney's front and left.

Time: nearly 4 P.M.

Despite retreat orders, Maj. Peter on Barney's left kept his guns firing as Barney and Col. Beall continued to hold the road to the capital against Ross's envelopment from three directions.

Col. Beall contested his hill as best he could, killing sixteen British, but finally abandoned it with four of his own dead.

As fast as Barney's gunners fell, others took their places from among the seamen acting as infantry. But when the commodore himself fell, a British musket ball in his hip, the end loomed.

Ross's redcoats swarmed up out of the ravine from all sides.

"Finding the enemy now completely in our rear and no means of defence," Barney reported, "I gave orders to my officers and men to retire."

Reluctantly, the sailors spiked their guns and fought their way out. At Barney's insistence, they left their fallen commodore behind one of his 18-pounders—to meet victorious Ross on the brightest spot of Bladensburg's battlefield.

5

FLAMES
IN WASHINGTON:
24 AUGUST 1814

I

At Winder's final order for American retreat from Bladensburg, "some shed tears, others uttered imprecations, and all evinced the utmost astonishment and indignation," said an eyewitness, "for it was impossible for them to comprehend why troops who were willing to risk an encounter with the enemy should be denied the opportunity."

As the general rode to Washington with Monroe and Gen. Armstrong, ahead of Gen. Smith's District and Georgetown troops, he met Col. Minor rushing hopefully to the battle with Virginia militia who finally had got their flints from a dilatory storekeeper. He turned them around and marched them back with the Columbians through the Capital toward Tennallytown on the Frederick road.

The British made no move to chase Winder's fleeing forces. As Cockburn reported to London: "The victors were too weary and the vanquished too swift."

Ross ordered a two-hour rest for his troops in the late afternoon's blazing heat. He personally saw to Com. Barney's medical care and parole, and set about burying some 100 of his dead on the field.

Though the Americans later found and buried some sixty more, Ross officially reported his Bladensburg losses as 56 killed, 185 wounded: Lieut. Gleig totaled casualties at 500; American estimates included 1,000 prisoners and deserters as well. Estimates of American losses ran from 10 to 40 killed and from 30 to 60 wounded, with 120 prisoners and 10 cannon left behind.

By the time the sun of 24 August began to set on Bladensburg, Ross had bivouacked and hospitalized most of his forces and, via Upper Marlboro, held open communication lines with Cochrane at Benedict.

Ross then went about the business that he and Cockburn had set their hearts on.

"To Rear-Admiral Cockburn who suggested the attack on Washington and who accompanied the army," he reported, "I confess the greatest obligation for his cordial co-operation and advice."

Forming a new brigade from his least tired men, Ross started some 1,500 redcoats over the District line toward the wide-open, undefended capital of the United States.

The general went ahead, with Cockburn, in an advanced party of 200. He had in mind, British officers with him believed, to deal with civil authorities and lay tribute on the city. But the American authorities, "officers of state and local magistrates, regardless of all but their personal safety, took to their heels by common consent and left the public buildings to their fate."

The capital's evacuation had started with arrival of the British at Upper Marlboro, 20 miles from Washington. Confusion had reigned, women and children running through the streets with bedding, clothes, and furniture while their men, with arms, joined their commands.

In the Department of State, which shared a building with the Department of War, Chief Clerk John Graham, Stephen

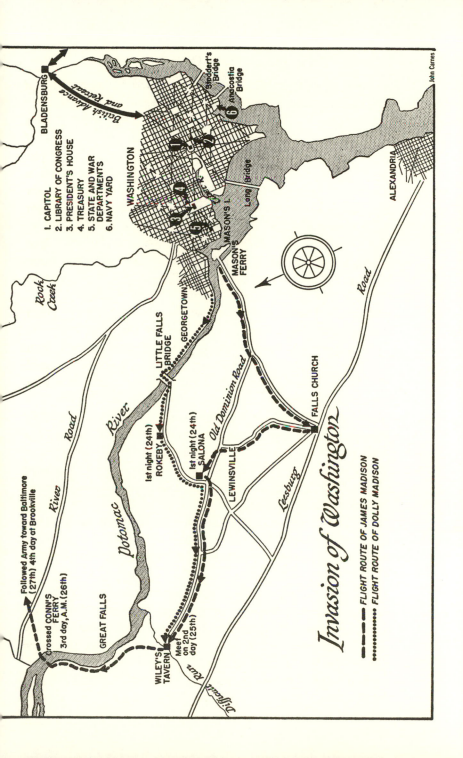

Invasion of Washington

1. CAPITOL
2. LIBRARY OF CONGRESS
3. PRESIDENT'S HOUSE
4. TREASURY
5. STATE AND WAR DEPARTMENTS
6. NAVY YARD

━ ━ ━ FLIGHT ROUTE OF JAMES MADISON
•••••• FLIGHT ROUTE OF DOLLY MADISON

John Carnes

Pleasanton, and Josiah King had gathered up and put into coarse linen sacks the public records of that department despite Gen. Armstrong's observation that he "did not think the British were serious in their intention of coming to Washington."

The documents included the parchment copy of the Declaration of Independence which Timothy Matlock of Philadelphia had engrossed, the Articles of Confederation, the Federal Constitution, many treaties, and Gen. Washington's commission as commander-in-chief of the Army of the Revolution (relinquished by Washington at Annapolis and found among the rubbish of a garret).

Pleasanton commandeered carts to move the bags to safety and, on 22 August, convoyed these national archives—including Revolutionary War records which had survived War Department and Treasury Department fires in 1800—across the long wooden Potomac River bridge to Edgar Patterson's Virginia gristmill. But Gen. John Mason's cannon foundry lay close to the mill on the Maryland side of the river; so, believing the enemy would surely seek to destroy the foundry, Pleasanton next day moved his national treasures farther into the interior and locked the documents in an unoccupied Leesburg house, 35 miles from Washington. Thus they rested, safe, as Ross and his invading redcoats marched down Maryland Avenue into the capital.

Soft golden clouds floated over the southern horizon and a pale moon glowed as the British came with a white flag to parley. But no American official appeared. Instead, a volley of musketry greeted Ross from Robert Sewall's 2nd Street house, rented by Albert Gallatin when Secretary of the Treasury. Bullets shot Ross's horse (third that day) under him, killed one soldier, wounded three others; and neither Ross nor Washington's officials ever found out whether some Barney men, a French barber, an Irish barber, or outraged civilians provided the greeting. Ross could only uncover a few unarmed Negroes hiding in nearby bushes.

After burning the house in reprisal, Ross encamped his troops in an open field east of the Capitol and waited for someone in authority to talk surrender terms and prize money for his expedition. Waiting, he saw flames down New Jersey Avenue where it ended in the Navy Yard.

The time: 8:20 P.M.

Com. Tingey, London-born British naval officer who served in the American Continental Navy during the Revolution and fought the French in America's 1799 Navy, had had a hard day at the Yard. Commandant since 1804, two years after its establishment, he had come to look on his home there as personal property. When, two days earlier, it had become apparent to him that the British intended to move on Washington, he had had Mordecai Booth, chief clerk, move powder and records to safety in Virginia.

On the morning of 24 August he had loaded wagons with munitions for Barney's guns. And at 2 P.M. he had Navy Secretary Jones's personal instructions to fire the Yard—not defend it—if the British came. All afternoon he had waited on tenterhooks while Booth sallied out of the Yard to glean what information he could from militia running, hobbling, creeping from Bladensburg. Booth could not vouch for the value of his intelligence and Tingey continued to hold off firing the Yard.

The burning of Stoddert's bridge the night previous, following Winder's retreat from Old Field, may have influenced Com. Tingey's determination to hold the Yard until the last possible moment. The bridge had gone up in flames unnecessarily. As one objective critic declared: "The enemy would have had no occasion to use it, and would not have carried it away as a trophy. But as all the materials had been got ready in the morning both to burn and blow it up, it was probably destroyed on the same principle which has induced some thrifty housewives, after a fit of sickness in the family, to swallow the medicine which was left in order to save money and prevent waste."

Pleas of nearby residents also shored up Com. Tingey's resolve to delay the torch, though he turned a deaf ear on the idea that he disregard the Secretary's order completely. Booth again went out to survey the situation.

When he returned—having seen advancing enemy troops and heard their shots overhead as he galloped back to the Yard, and having found the city's streets otherwise empty in the heavy air of an oncoming storm—Com. Tingey pulled out his watch, observed it read 8:20, and ordered the Yard fired.

When, in the heavy evening calm, seamen applied matches to the trains of Dupont powder which ignited inflammable material strategically placed, the fire did not carry to neighboring property. But in a few moments the flames took hold of the Yard and, as Com. Tingey reported to Secretary Jones, "the whole was in a state of irretrievable conflagration."

New frigate *Columbia*, ready for coppering, could have gone down the ways in ten days; sloop *Argus* lay at the wharf with all her armament and equipment on board except her sails, provisions, and powder. Both vessels roared quickly into a sheet of fire that took in the Yard's shops, lofts, machinery, and tools—along with the hulls of old frigates *Boston* and *General Greene*.

Among the seamen who saw the Yard ignominiously go up into flames watched a former Mediterranean Sea pilot, a Maltese. Now Gunner Salvadore Catalano of the United States Navy, in 1803 he had sailed Stephen Decatur, Thomas Macdonough, and other naval greats—now defeating the British on the Atlantic Ocean and the Great Lakes—into Tripoli harbor. Under the guns of enemy Turks, Catalano had helped burn frigate *Philadelphia* in what Nelson called the "boldest act of the age." A far cry from this fire!

"From a momentary impulse and faint hope of recovering" new schooner *Lynx*, near completion, Com. Tingey set no torch to that vessel and quitted the wharf in his gig. Headed down the Eastern Branch toward Alexandria, he heard the Greenleaf Point fort roar as it too went up in flames.

To Ross, fruitlessly waiting for a parley on tribute, the Navy Yard flames may have suggested his next actions. With Cockburn he talked over Admiralty instructions to put all American military and public property to the torch in order to prevent "a repetition of the uncivilized proceedings of the troops of the United States." Cockburn urged burning the entire city; Ross consented to burning public buildings.

They began with the Capitol and, as Midshipman Lovell commented, "the blaze that burnt York reached Washington."

British soldiers fired a volley through the windows of Congress House and broke into the Hall of Representatives. Here Ross and Cockburn found an apartment as "incomparably more vast and splendid than their dark and crowded Commons chapel of St. Stephens as the American Senate Chamber is a much more imposing spectacle than their old House of Lords."

American congressmen later related that Cockburn began this pyromaniacal night by mounting the Speaker's chair and putting the question to assembled redcoats: "Shall this harbor of Yankee democracy be burned? All for it will say, Aye."

True or false, none of Cockburn's broad humor showed in any of Ross's actions; reports aver that he did not smile once during his stay in Washington.

"The difference in the manners of the two," Maj. Williams suggests, "was probably the usual difference between officers of the navy and army in the British service; Cockburn, as the sailor, may have been the more frank and generous of the two, notwithstanding his rudeness of manner."

Niles' Weekly Register, pointing out that Ross headed the expedition, asked:

Why, then, should the conflagration be charged to Cockburn? In a homely proverb, *exactly* suited to this occasion, "Give the devil his due."

Ross made the burning—carried out, according to historian Benjamin J. Lossing, under Lieutenant George Pratt, second of *Sea Horse*—a subject of boasting.

"There was no want of materials for the conflagration," reports Benjamin H. Latrobe, who had taken over the Capitol's design from Dr. Thornton in 1803, "for when the number of members of Congress was increased the old platform was left in its place and another raised over it, giving an additional quantity of dry and loose lumber. All the stages and seats of the galleries were of timber and yellow pine. The mahogany desks, tables, and chairs were in their places.

"At first rockets were fired through the roof, but they did not set fire to it. They sent men on it, but it was covered with sheet iron. At last they made a great pile in the center of the room of furniture and, retiring, set fire to a quantity of rocket stuff in the middle. The whole was soon in a blaze, and so intense was the flame that the glass of the lights was melted, and I have now lamps weighing many pounds run into a mass."

The Senate wing blazed similarly, and the temporary wooden structure that connected House and Senate took fire even more rapidly. Nearby homes, including one owned by George Washington, went up in the inferno that consumed the Library of Congress (holding 3,000 volumes and 50-odd maps and charts) and all but one cartload of legislative records.

The President of the United States—riding over the Virginia countryside with his Attorney General in the company of Gen. Mason, Charles Carroll of Bellevue, and ropewalk owner Tench Ringgold—glimpsed the sparks and flames mounting high up in the dark.

"If at intervals the dismal sight was lost to our view," Rush said later, "we got it again from some hilltop or eminence where we paused to look at it."

The British intended the Capitol's complete destruction.

The exterior of columns and entablature scaled off; and not a vestige of sculpture or fluting remained. But the greater part of the freestone exterior and the principal divisions of the interior resisted the flames.

Then, records Congressman Charles Jared Ingersoll:

"The Capitol wrapped in its winding sheet of fire, the troops slightly refreshed after that first perpetration were led by the General and Admiral along, then, almost the only thoroughfare of Washington—the eternal Pennsylvania Avenue—without beat of drum or other martial sound than their ponderous tramp, a mile and a quarter towards the President's House, the Treasury and War Offices, to burn them."

As he marched down the avenue at the head of a small detachment, Ross had much to disquiet him:

Winder might gather forces to fall on his soldiers; poisoned water and food might decimate his troops; the British Potomac fleet might not get up to Alexandria to support him; Baltimore troops might march on his tired and wounded in Bladensburg. At the head of a second detachment three or four blocks behind, Cockburn on muleback appeared exhilarated by the night's activities, however.

The general and the admiral halted at the long, low brick lodginghouse of aging Mistress Suter whose two sons earlier had stopped here—one wounded with Barney—in flight from Bladensburg. Here, close to the President's House and directly opposite the Treasury, Ross entered and announced himself to the unhappy hostess as having "come to sup with you."

And while Mrs. Suter and her woman servant went out into the yard and kitchen to kill fowls and warm bread for the suppers of twelve unwelcome guests, Ross and Cockburn went across the street to visit the President's Palace.

The time: between 9 and 10 P.M.

2

AT THE PRESIDENT'S HOUSE that morning of 24 August, after her husband had left to counsel with his Cabinet at the Navy

Yard, Dolly Madison received an understated note from the Navy Secretary's wife:

My Dear Madam,

In the present state of alarm, I imagine it will be more convenient to dispense with the enjoyment of your hospitality today, and therefore pray you to admit this as an excuse for Mr. Jones, Lucy and myself. Mr. Jones is deeply engaged in dispatching the marines and attending to the public duties. . . .

Yours very truly and affectionately,
E. Jones

Outside the House, a hot sun burned on the swamps; inside, Dolly Madison packed.

"I confess," she wrote to Mrs. Latrobe later, "that I was so un-feminine as to be free from fear, and willing to remain in the *Castle* if I could have had a cannon through every window. . . ."

Early that day she did have a guard of 100 men under Colonel Daniel Carroll, but they went to fight at Bladensburg.

Inside the House, while she took time to write installments of a letter to her sister, Mrs. George Steptoe Washington, at Mount Vernon, Jean P. Sioussa helped gather together and pack what Dolly Madison hoped to save if she had to flee. ("French John" had jumped ship, frigate *Didon*, in 1804 to become father of six American children and doorkeeper to the Madisons.) They gathered papers and memoranda from the President's desk, pressing "as many cabinet papers into trunks as to fill one carriage." Dolly Madison also packed silver, books, velvet curtains, even a small clock, but none of her or her husband's personal effects except for a few of his clothes.

All day long she turned her spyglass in every direction, "watching with unwearied anxiety, hoping to discover the approach of my dear husband and his friends; but, alas, I can descry only groups of military wandering in all directions, as if there was a lack of arms or of spirit to fight for their own firesides." Mayor James H. Blake came twice to warn her of her own danger, but she would not leave the President's House.

"Mrs. Madison ordered dinner to be ready at 3, as usual," writes serving boy Paul Jennings. "I set the table myself, and brought up the ale, cider, and wine, and placed them in the coolers, as all the cabinet and several military gentlemen and strangers were expected."

While she waited, the First Lady also tended to the George Washington portrait that hung on the dining room's west wall. George W. P. Custis, grandson of Martha Washington had called the day before seeking to save it, and Dolly Madison had no intention of leaving it for the British.

Copied by Jane Stuart from the original her father painted for William Bingham of "Landsdowne" on the west bank of the Schuylkill River, it hung in a heavy external gilt frame. Stuart had done the original head; Winstanley had filled in the body, limbs, posture, and manner of Washington, using for his model President John Adams's son-in-law, William Smith.

Unable to unscrew the ornate frame from the wall, Dolly Madison sent Thomas McGaw, her Irish gardener, for a hatchet. But while the gardener looked for the hatchet, French John got the canvas out, intact on its inner frame.

To shipowner Jacob Barker and Robert G. L. DePeyster of New York, who stopped to ask if they could help, the First Lady turned over the portrait. They carted it through Georgetown to Montgomery Court House and deposited it for safekeeping "with a widow lady at a country house some distance from the road." Six weeks later Barker delivered it to the Secretary of State for varnishing, a new outer frame, and eventual reinstatement in the President's House.

At 3 P.M. Dolly Madison added to her sister's note:

"Mr. Madison comes not; may God protect him! Two messengers, covered with dust, come to bid me fly; but I wait for him. . . ."

Finally, writes Jennings, "James Smith, a free colored man who had accompanied Mr. Madison to Bladensburg, galloped up to the House, waving his hat, and cried out, 'Clear out, clear out! Gen. Armstrong has ordered a retreat!'"

With this news, Smith also brought the First Lady a penciled note from the President, directing her to fly at once.

She ordered her carriage and, says Jennings, "passing through the dining room caught up what silver she could crowd into her old-fashioned reticule, and then jumped into the chariot with her servant girl Sukey and Daniel Carroll who took charge of them; Jo. Bolin drove them over to Georgetown Heights." In the coach French John had piled boxes and bags he helped pack that morning.

Jennings reports that the President's directive for the First Lady to flee brought instant confusion. This lasted for some time, with conflicting reports of what happened. Among these happenings:

A few minutes after Dolly Madison's departure, French John provided refreshments for the President's party which stopped by briefly . . . after they, in turn, left, he set before the door buckets of water and bottles of wine for some of Col. Laval's dragoons, some regular troops, and a company or two of volunteers from the Bladensburg battlefield . . . during the hubbub, someone "lifted" the Campbell duelling pistols which Madison had carried to Bladensburg and removed from their holsters while he ate . . . and, says Jennings, "a rabble, taking advantage of the confusion, ran all over the House and stole lots of silver and whatever they could lay their hands on."

What foods and wines remained in the mansion after the President's party, Col. Laval's dragoons, and the rabble departed has served for 150 years of international debate.

A warm and generous hostess, Dolly Madison took pride in the table she set and, for the previous week, had held what amounted to open house, with food laid out for all who called on the President. A foreign minister earlier had remarked that one of her dinners seemed "more like a harvest-home supper than the entertainment of a secretary of state" to which she had countered that the profusion so repugnant to foreign customs arose from "the happy circumstance of the super-abundance and prosperity of our country." She did not, she said, "hesitate to sacrifice the delicacy of European taste for the less elegant but more liberal fashion of Virginia."

When Dolly Madison departed from the mansion that afternoon she left behind a well-stocked larder and wine cellar.

Paul Jennings had set the table for three o'clock dinner and had laid much of the dinner out, in addition to the ale, cider, and wine in the coolers.

And after he saw the last of the uninvited guests out, delivered the mansion's macaw into the hands of the French Ambassador's cook at Col. Tayloe's Octagon House a quarter-mile distant, and returned—French John must have extinguished all fires before he locked up and hied himself off to the security of Russian Minister Daschkoff's residence.

Cockburn dominated the scene at the President's House that night while Mistress Suter prepared supper across the way.

When the British broke into "Jemmy's Palace," as the jocose admiral took pleasure in dubbing it, he corraled a local book dealer for guide and rambled through the mansion. Surveying what, he told young Richard Weightman, he must presently "give to the flames," he picked out souvenirs—among them an old *chapeau bras* of James Madison's and a chair cushion of Dolly Madison's.

Sitting down with the uncomfortable book dealer, Cockburn drank a toast to Jemmy's health while soldiers and sailors ransacked the mansion from cellar to garret.

Upstairs, Lieut. Scott hastily visited "the beautiful apartments" and:

"Passing through the President's dressing-room (which from its disordered state, opened drawers, and half-filled portmanteaus must have been abandoned in the midst of packing up), the snowy clean linen tempted me to take the liberty of making a very fair exchange. I accordingly doffed my inner garment, and thrust my unworthy person into a shirt belonging to no less a personage than the chief magistrate of the United States."

The redcoats found little of value except for a small parcel of penciled notes which the President had sent the First Lady while in the field with the troops, but they had themselves a frolic. And they ate.

"We found a supper all ready," Harry Smith reported, "which was sufficiently cooked without more fire, and which many of us speedily consumed, unaided by the fiery elements, and drank some very good wine also." Ross counted covers for forty.

Thus the President's three o'clock dinner, uncleared by household servants in the confusion of the afternoon's alarms, served as a cold buffet for Bladensburg's victors.

"Nor was Mr. Madison's health forgotten, in his own best claret," another British officer wrote home, "for being such a good fellow as to leave us such a capital supper."

Having savored the table of the nation's first hostess, Ross sent to a small beerhouse opposite the Treasury for fire. Awaiting it, the soldiers and sailors collected in the drawing room all the furniture they could find. The fire arrived from Frenchy Nardin's saloon.

The time: 11 P.M.

To Ross goes credit for the order to ignite the piled-up furniture; to Cockburn goes credit for the skill with which his men did the job—again, says Lossing, under Lieut. Pratt of *Sea Horse*.

"I shall never forget the destructive majesty of the flames," Harry Smith declared, "as the torches were applied to beds, curtains, etc. Our sailors were artists at the work."

Flames leaped from yellow damask to polished mahogany, raged up Jefferson's grand staircase, and poured skyward through the roof in a conflagration seen for thirty miles. Cockburn always burned, Harry Smith reveals, "with the ruthless firebrand of the Red Savages of the woods."

Furniture, books, pictures, wines, provisions, and family belongings which had cost the Madisons $12,000 fed a fire that left "unroofed naked walls, cracked, defaced and blackened."

Delighted with his visit to Jemmy's palace, Cockburn finally hoisted himself onto his mule and rode partly through Mrs. Suter's front door to supper. Blowing out the table's candles, he jovially told his companions that he preferred to eat by the light of the burning palace—and of the nearby Treasury which, meanwhile, Ross had fired. When a fellow officer asked if the pair hadn't one other building to burn—the War Department—Cockburn replied, "Certainly."

Ross demurred. "It will be time enough in the morning," he said, "as it is now growing late, and the men require rest."

But when Ross assembled his detachment after supper to march back to their Capitol Hill camp, Cockburn stopped at the office of the *National Intelligencer* to look for Editor Gales who, he advised some men who directed him, "has been telling some tough stories about me." He considered firing the office then and there. But two women who lived in the adjoining house prevailed on him to forgo that pleasure.

Riding through the heavy rainstorm that now pelted Washington and helped contain the city's fires, Cockburn inadvertently left behind at the *Intelligencer* office a sentry placed on the street when the detachment halted there. Pacing his Pennsylvania Avenue post a mile away from where Ross's invading army tried to sleep in their sodden encampment on the other side of gutted Congress House, this single redcoat guarded the captured city all night for the British.

While Dolly Madison rode through the storming dark in search of her husband, while James Madison sought to elude British capture, while James Monroe scoured the countryside endeavoring to reassemble troops and cut off Ross's retreat to his ships, while William Winder rounded up stragglers at Montgomery Court House, and while Washington's citizens "spent the night in gazing on the fires and lamenting the disgrace of the city," Robert Ross and George Cockburn called it a day.

The triumphant general rode to his quarters in Dr. James Ewell's home and the conquering admiral, Ingersoll relates, "concluded his victorious and destructive orgies of that memorable day with the coarse luxury of lust in a brothel. . . ."

3

THE BRITISH roused themselves early on the morning of Thursday 25 August to greet a sultry dawn and the havoc they and the storm had wreaked the night before.

Up at 5:30 A.M., Cockburn found himself a gray mare and went out on the town with a black colt trotting behind. After early breakfast at Dr. Ewell's, Ross hopefully scanned the Potomac for a reassuring glimpse of Capt. Gordon's support fleet. Admiral and general then resumed their arson.

At 8 A.M. Cockburn and Capt. Wainwright of *Tonnant* arrived at the Navy Yard where their seamen set fire to unburned buildings and stores while their officers mutilated the Tripoli monument. They had moved on to destroy Tench Ringgold, Heath & Company's and John Chalmers's ropewalks when Com. Tingey arrived at the Yard by gig from Alexandria at 8:45 to find neighborhood vultures plundering his own unharmed home and that of the Marine commandant. Cochrane, friends told Com. Tingey, had expressed a particular desire to take him captive.

At 8 A.M., from Capitol Hill's smoke-blackened sandstone ruins, Ross marched some 900 men in three detachments—each followed by about thirty Negroes carrying rockets and combustibles—down quiet Pennsylvania Avenue to where the roofless President's House smoldered.

Flames had made little headway, however, against the

Treasury before the previous night's storm. So Ross fired that building again. He then fired the War and State Department building and moved on to the only unburned public structure—old three-story reconverted Blodget's Hotel which housed the Post Office Department and the State Department's Patent Bureau.

As the British stood with axes at the building's doors, waiting for Major Waters to give the word to chop their way in, Dr. Thornton—first chief of patents as well as designer of Congress House—came up. His personal and patriotic anger had mounted with every flame ascending the previous night's sky from the Capitol; figuratively, almost literally, he now burned at this fresh outrage which threatened the patent models entrusted to his custody.

With fervor that carried through his stammering, he told the major: "Are you Englishmen or vandals? . . . This is a depository of the American nation in which the whole of the civilized world is interested. . . ."

As the nonplused officer hesitated, Dr. Thornton's words continued to ring out: ". . . nothing but private property of any consequence . . . any public property to which the major objected might be burnt in the street, provided the building might be preserved . . . hundreds of models of the arts, impossible to remove . . . to burn what would be useful to all mankind would be as barbarous as formerly to burn the Alexandrian Library, for which the Turks have been ever since condemned by all enlightened nations. . . ."

Like Com. Barney, Dr. Thornton stood up to the enemy. And in the end the British moved away, leaving him a hero and the Patents Bureau unharmed.

Down at the Potomac River bridge another American also stopped the British practically singlehanded. On the Virginia side of the mile-long bridge, this corporal and his guard "perceiving a body of the British ready to pass over, concluded the surest and best method to prevent it was to destroy by fire that end and part where he was posted." And the

British, on the Washington side of the river, expecting an attack from the corporal's "large American force," fired their end!

During that second day of the invasion and capture of Washington, Cockburn took his pound of flesh from the *National Intelligencer* for a year's deriding. He had long nursed a desire to lay his hands on Joseph Gales, but the editor had gone out days ago with Winder's army to report from the field; and, the morning before the Bladensburg battle, the entire staff of the "confidential journal of Mr. Madison's administration" had joined their militia companies. On his second visit to the newspaper office, Cockburn therefore had only cold type to work with, and he proved no match for his American critic in the use of that—he could only pi it.

"Be sure," he told his men as they moved inside to smash the presses into scrap iron, "that all the *C*'s in the boxes are destroyed so that the rascals can have no further means of abusing my name."

Grossly delighted, he also watched his men throw the *Intelligencer*'s library of several hundred books into the street where, eyewitnesses reported, "the harlequin of havoc" helped in their burning.

Closing hours of the Ross-Cockburn Washington frolic went badly for the British.

At 2 P.M. a detachment of 200 redcoats, with several officers, marched to Greenleaf Point to finish off the arsenal and one or two other buildings which the Americans only partially had destroyed on the preceding night. Before leaving the Point, the Americans had concealed a large quantity of kegged powder in a dry-well near the barracks.

"One of our artillerymen," reported a surviving British officer, "most unfortunately dropped a lighted port-fire into the well which, with a magazine about twelve yards distant, full of shells charged and primed, blew up with the most tremendous explosion I ever heard. One house was unroofed and the walls of two others, which had been burnt an hour before, were shook down.

"Large pieces of earth, stones, bricks, shot, shells, etc., burst into the air and, falling among us (who had nowhere to run, being on a narrow neck of land), killed about twelve men and wounded above thirty more, most of them in a dreadful manner . . . the groans of the people almost buried in the earth, or with legs and arms broke, and the sight of bodies lying about, was a thousand times more distressing than the loss we met in the field the day before."

While the redcoats, still stunned by this shocking calamity, carried their writhing wounded to a hospital which Ross set up in a house near the Capitol, a terrifying (to the British) storm struck.

"Of the prodigious force of the wind it is impossible for you to form any conception," Lieut. Gleig declares. "Roofs of houses were torn off by it, and whisked into the air like sheets of paper; while the rain which accompanied it resembled the rushing of a mighty cataract rather than the dropping of a shower.

"The darkness was as great as if the sun had long set and the last remains of twilight had come on, occasionally relieved by flashes of vivid lightning streaming through it; which, together with the noise of the wind and the thunder, the crash of falling buildings, and the tearing of roofs as they were stript from the walls, produced the most appalling effect I ever have, and probably ever shall, witness.

"This lasted for nearly two hours without intermission, during which time many of the houses spared by us were blown down and thirty of our men, besides several of the inhabitants, buried beneath their ruins.

"Our column was as completely dispersed as if it had received a total defeat, some of the men flying for shelter behind walls and buildings and others falling flat upon the ground to prevent themselves from being carried away by the tempest; nay, such was the violence of the wind that two pieces of cannon which stood upon the eminence were fairly lifted from the ground and borne several yards to the rear."

During their occupation of the capital, the British did not go beyond a line of sentinels between the Treasury and the President's House. They left Georgetown undisturbed. But they went far enough to suit Ross.

Besides the volley that had greeted his entry into the city, his troops had encountered only one armed man, John Lewis, grandnephew of George Washington. Impressed at sea, Lewis had escaped, vowing vengeance; he had taken it, the night before, by firing at British sentinels who shot him dead.

Now, without sign of Capt. Gordon's Potomac fleet, with rumors of 12,000 Virginia and 15,000 Maryland troops massing to come down on him in retaliation, with his soldiers running into such booby traps as at Greenleaf Point, with a two-hour hurricane scaring the wits out of his men, and having burned the capital to a shambles and picked up considerable booty, Ross decided to end the occupation.

At 8 P.M., leaving Capitol Hill's campfires burning brightly, he quietly withdrew.

"Officers of the different corps had been directed, in a whisper, to make ready for falling back as soon as darkness should set in," Lieut. Gleig discloses. "From the men, however, the thing was kept profoundly secret. They were given to understand that an important maneuver would be effected before morning, but the hints thrown out tended to induce an expectation of a further advance rather than a retreat.

"A similar rumor was permitted quietly to circulate among the inhabitants with the view, doubtless, of its making its way into the American camp; while all persons were required, on pain of death, to keep within doors from sunset to sunrise."

Harry Smith protested retiring in what he considered a most injudicious manner. He had been out in the camp and, when he returned after dark, General Ross told him:

"I have ordered the army to march at night."

"Tonight?" Harry Smith said. "I hope not, sir. The road,

you well know, for four miles to Bladensburg is excellent and wide enough to march with a front of subdivisions. After that we have to move through woods by a track, not a road. Let us move so as to reach Bladensburg by daylight. Our men will have a night's rest, and be refreshed after the battle. I have also to load all the wounded and to issue flour, which I have also caused to be collected."

He had seized in Washington everything in the shape of transport.

The general replied: "I have made the arrangement with Evans, and we must march."

Says Harry Smith: "I muttered to myself. . . ."

The British retreat looked more forlorn than martial, Dr. Hanson Catlett, regular U. S. Army surgeon, reveals.

"They . . . had about forty miserable-looking horses haltered up, ten or twelve carts and wagons, one ox-cart, one coachee, and several gigs. . . . A drove of sixty or seventy cattle preceded this cavalcade."

"Large quantities of fresh fuel were heaped upon the fires," says Lieut. Gleig; "while from every company a few men were selected who should remain beside them till the pickets withdrew and move from time to time about so that their figures might be seen by the light of the blaze. After this the troops stole to the rear of the fires by twos and threes. When far enough removed to avoid observation, they took their places and, in profound silence, began their march.

"The night was very dark. Stars there were in the sky but, for some time after quitting the light of the bivouac, their influence was wholly unfelt. We moved on, however, in good order. No man spoke above his breath, our very steps were planted lightly, and we cleared the town without exciting observation."

Ross marched his invaders rapidly and in good order to Bladensburg, where he loaded his battle wounded. But after a tedious trek through woods "as dark as chaos," the British got only 3 miles out of Bladensburg.

"Our soldiers were dead done and so fatigued there was nothing for it but to halt," Harry Smith confesses, "while we staff were looking out, like a lieutenant of the navy in chase, to see the Yankees come down upon us with showers of sharpshooters. Thanks to their kind consideration they abstained from doing so, but we were very much in their power."

In four days, Ross covered the remaining miles to Benedict, rejoining Cochrane on Monday 29 August.

"We reached our landing place unmolested and at our leisure embarked our army which," Harry Smith discloses, "began to suffer very much from dysentery."

By *Intelligencer* estimates, his expedition had cost Ross some 1,000 men—200 killed and upwards of 400 wounded in battle and explosion, many dead of fatigue, numbers taken prisoners by cavalry hanging on his rear, and "not a few deserted."

But in ten days he had marched 4,500 troops some 50 miles into the heartland of 10,000,000 Americans, defeated their army, sacked their capital in reprisal for the burning of Upper Canada's, and safely marched 50 miles back to his shipping with 540 barrels of powder, 206 cannons, and 100,000 rounds of cartridges listed as captured.

With Cockburn, Ross had humiliated the American nation.

4

As Ross ENTERED the Patuxent to start his epic overland march on Washington, Captain James Alexander Gordon—not yet thirty years old, a leg lost in Britain's Adriatic fighting—set out on an equally amazing water expedition against the American capital.

With some 1,004 "ships companies [total complement] by no means fit to cope with the picked men of America," Capt. Gordon on 17 August went about manhandling 38-gun frigate *Sea Horse*, 36-gun *Euryalus* with Captain Charles Napier as the squadron's second-in-command, three bomb vessels—

Aetna, Devastation, Meteor; rocket-ship *Erebus,* and dispatch boat *Anna Maria* up the Potomac River.

American frigate *President,* 44, once had come downriver from Washington in some forty-two days, her guns taken out in order to float her over the Potomac's extensive shoals. A British frigate already had abandoned, as impossible, efforts to effect an upriver passage. And, if he ever reached so high, Capt. Gordon had a fort to pass on Mason's Island—6 miles below Alexandria, 12 below Washington.

The second day brought him above the Wicomico River to the Kettle Bottoms, intricate shoals "composed of oyster banks of various dimensions, some not larger than a boat, with passages between them." Admiralty charts of 1776 helped little; "none of the pilots know exactly where they lie."

With no pilot, *Sea Horse* led along the Virginia shore, *Euryalus* and the squadron following. Capt. Napier's own words paint the most vivid picture of their incredible voyage:

"The wind was light, and several boats ahead sounding. As long as the soundings were good, no apprehension was entertained; being aware of the smallness of the obstructions, it appeared impossible, if the ship ahead found a passage, that those astern could not be brought up. We were, however, mistaken: the *Euryalus* opened the ball and struck or, rather, was suddenly brought up, for nothing was felt, and the lead gave us plenty of water. The signal was made to anchor, and boats and hawsers were sent to assist in getting her off.

"No one could tell where she hung. There was abundance of water astern, ahead, all round, and yet the ship was immovable. A diver went down and found, to the astonishment of all on board, that an oyster bank, not bigger than a boat, was under the bilge. The boats had missed it with the lead, and the *Sea Horse* had passed perhaps by a few feet on one side."

After some hard heaving, *Euryalus* floated and the squadron again weighed. It proceeded with great caution, sending —ahead of the ships—several boats abreast of one another to sound with lead lines. Despite this care, *Sea Horse* grounded on a sandbank.

"The tide appeared flowing and no difficulty was anticipated, but she was immovable. A strict examination showed that, though the tide was apparently running up, the water was diminishing. Not until it had flowed several hours was there any perceptible increase of depth. Her water was started and a great part of her provisions and eight or ten guns were hoisted out before she floated. Several of the other ships were also ashore, but got off with more ease."

Sea Horse's crew spent 18 August getting in her provisions and guns, sounding the channel, and preparing to warp in the event of a foul wind.

Next day the squadron again weighed, with a favorable breeze, and before dark cleared the Kettle Bottoms without serious difficulty, each vessel acting independently and picking her way to the best of her commander's judgment. All ships grounded occasionally, but none as hard as had *Sea Horse*.

The wind being foul on the morning of 20 August, Capt. Gordon signaled to warp.

Each ship divided her boats into two divisions, one division handling the stream anchor, the other the kedge. As Capt. Napier describes these back-breaking labors, "The stream was first laid out, and all the hawsers bent to it; and as the ship was warped ahead the hawsers were coiled in the boats of the second division, which laid out the kedge; and it was so arranged that the end should be on board as the other anchor became short, stay, or peak.

"When the tide was favourable and wind light, we warped by hand; with the ebb and wind strong, the hawsers were brought to the capstan. This operation began at daylight and was carried on without interruption till dark, and lasted five days during which the squadron warped upwards of fifty miles."

On the first day, the evening of 24 August, the squadron anchored off Maryland Point. From their decks the British saw, in the sky over Washington, the reflection of the burning Capitol and President's House. Believing Ross had put the torch to the city at the moment of evacuating it, and disappointed not to have participated in the invasion of the American capital, Capt. Gordon and his staff nevertheless decided to proceed on their own upriver thrust.

With the next reach, though very shoal, sufficiently wide to beat through, officers and men looked forward to relaxation from their exertions. For they not only had warped by day but, at night, had rowed their boats on guard in every direction. Thus far they had not piped down their hammocks. They hoped, too, that the Americans would continue to give no trouble, either with fire vessels or with troops which, the British thought, might have been stationed along the river on both banks to make it totally impossible for the squadron to lay out anchors.

"Considering we were several hundred miles in the interior of an enemy's country, the utmost precaution was necessary to provide against any unforeseen attack. The strictest discipline was observed in the guard boats: no landing or plundering was permitted—the numerous flocks of geese swam undisturbed in the river—the bullocks and sheep browsed unmolested—the poultry yards were respected, and any act that might irritate the inhabitants was most sedulously avoided."

Only once did a boat land during the night, in search of stock; and an American householder wounded one British seaman, "which served as a salutary example to the rest."

During the day of 24 August Capt. Napier went on shore with a flag of truce at an agreeable-looking residence—the first, he relates, that the invaders had seen close to the river.

"The owner was an American farmer—not the most polished man in the world. He had two daughters, rather homely, and uncouth as himself. They 'guessed' we would not go farther than Maryland Point, as the water was shoal; seemed to know and care very little about what was going on; offered us a glass of peach brandy, and hoped the 'Britishers' would not carry off their Negroes, which appeared to be their only apprehension."

The squadron weighed on the morning of 25 August and beat up Maryland Reach in about the depth of water the frigates drew—but sometimes less—dragging through the soft bottom. Of a sudden, shortly before noon, the sky became overcast, a squall making up. Newcomers to the Chesapeake had heard much of the violence of these northwest gusts, but Capt. Napier considered the reports exaggerated. He was not quite so cautious as he ought to have been, though he took in topgallant sails, mainsail, jib, and spanker.

"The squall thickened at a short distance, roaring in a most awful manner and appearing like a tremendous surf," he relates. "No time was to be lost: everything was clued up at the moment it reached us. Nevertheless we were nearly on our beam ends.

"A couple of anchors were let go and, as we swung to the wind, the bowsprit rose right up. This slackened the stays and away went the heads of all three topmasts; this saved the foremast which, in another moment, would have fallen. The bowsprit, being relieved, sunk back to its place but broke completely through."

Sea Horse sprung her mizzenmast; *Meteor*, lying on a bank, "was fairly blown over it and brought up in deep water." The entire squadron, which was all together with the exception of two vessels 4 or 5 miles lower down the river, suffered more or less.

"Capt. Gordon thought the game was up, but he was assured we should be refitted before the other ships joined."

Euryalus piped to dinner, leaving the wreckage as it lay. At 1:30 P.M. the hands were called, the wreckage cleared, bowsprit hoisted on board, a new one made out of topmast, and new crosstrees and trestletrees cut and fitted. Although the frigate's seamen did not work after dark, next day at 1 P.M. they reported *Euryalus* all a-taut, and she weighed as the two sternmost vessels passed.

"It was calm and the boats, manned with marines, towed the ship as the seamen were setting up the rigging."

With wind fair on 26 August, the squadron made all sail up the river which now assumed a more pleasing aspect because of the easy going. At 5 P.M George Washington's Mount Vernon home opened to view "and showed us, for the first time since we entered the Potomac, a gentleman's residence." In salute, the ships lowered fore-topsails; their bands played Washington's march.

Higher up the river, on the opposite side, Fort Washington appeared to anxious British eyes. Capt. Gordon considered it assailable, and a little before sunset the squadron anchored just out of gunshot. To cover the frigates in a projected attack at daylight next morning, the bomb vessels at once took up positions and began throwing shells.

Since July of 1813 Washington citizens generally had believed Fort Warburton, built in 1808 and renamed Fort Washington in 1813, to be "in a state of perfect defence. . . ." On the Maryland side of the river at the foot of a steep acclivity, with water battery and rear battery, it boasted an octagonal brick blockhouse two stories high. But this, "calculated against musketry only, could have been knocked down by a 12-pounder," said one general, and Winder, too, considered Fort Washington untenable.

The night before Bladensburg Winder had ordered its commanding officer, Captain Samuel T. Dyson, in event of "being taken in the rear of the fort by the enemy, to blow up the fort and retire across the river" with his 60-man garrison.

As the British bomb vessels began their bombardment, Capt. Dyson's garrison, to the attackers' great surprise, as Capt. Napier watched, "retreated from the fort; and, a short time after, Fort Washington was blown up—which left the capital of America, and the populous town of Alexandria, open to the squadron without the loss of a man."

Darkness prevented the British from knowing whether one of their own shells had demolished the fort or the garrison had sacrificed it. Opinion favored the latter, but the attackers found themselves "at a loss to account for such an extraordinary step." The fort held a good position, and its capture would have cost the British at least fifty men or more had it been properly defended. Too, even had the British succeeded in next morning's attack, they could—at worst—only have destroyed the fort.

"Dyson either misunderstood Winder's order or was scared," records Lossing. "He blew up and abandoned the fort without firing a gun."

Capt. Dyson declared he had had information that 6,000 enemy marched on the fort to co-operate with the British fleet.

In any event, Fort Washington did not hinder Capt. Gordon's invasion.

"At daylight the ships moored under the battery and completed its destruction," says Capt. Napier. "The guns were spiked by the enemy; we otherwise mutilated them and destroyed the carriages."

Fort Washington, he found, had a most respectable defense; it mounted two 32-pounders, eight 24-pounders; in a battery on the beach were five 18-pounders; in a martello tower, two 12-pounders, with loopholes for musketry; and a battery in the rear mounted two 12- and six 6-pound fieldpieces.

When, following the fall of Fort Washington, a deputation of Alexandria's townsmen approached to talk capitulation, Capt. Gordon declined to enter into any arrangements until his squadron arrived before Alexandria.

"The channel was buoyed," says Capt. Napier, "and, next morning, the 27th, we anchored abreast of the town."

5

SINCE MAY OF 1813 Alexandria had protested its defenselessness to an administration which replied, with undeniable truth, that it was "impossible to extend protection to every assailable point of the country."

Alexandria remained wholly neglected except for its own efforts. Even its local militia, swept into the capital's general defense at Ross's approach, had moved out of town. Alexandria thus faced Capt. Gordon's invading fleet with old men, women, and children armed with pitchforks, pokers, tongs, and brickbats.

Wanting no repetition of British excesses at Hampton, where civilians resisted, Alexandria's Common Council capitulated—on terms that gave Capt. Gordon the kind of tribute Ross had hoped to obtain from Washington:

> The town of Alexandria (with the exception of public works) shall not be destroyed, unless hostilities are commenced on the part of the Americans, nor shall the inhabitants be molested in any manner whatever, or their dwelling-houses entered, if the following articles are complied with:
>
> ARTICLE 1. All naval and ordnance stores (public and private) must be immediately given up.
>
> ART. 2. Possession will be immediately taken of all the shipping, and their furniture must be sent on board by their owners without delay.
>
> ART. 3. The vessels which have been sunk must be delivered up in the state they were in on the 19th of August, the day of the squadron passing the Kettle Bottoms.
>
> ART. 4. Merchandise of every description must be instantly delivered up, and to prevent any irregularities that might be committed in its embarkation, the merchants have it on their option to load the vessels generally employed for that purpose, when they will be towed off by us.
>
> ART. 5. All merchandise that has been removed from Alexandria since the 19th instant is to be included in the above articles.
>
> ART. 6. Refreshments of every description to be supplied the ships, and paid for at the market price by bills on the British government.

ART. 7. Officers will be appointed to see that the articles Nos. 2, 3, 4, and 5 are strictly complied with, and any deviation or non-compliance on the part of the inhabitants of Alexandria, will render this treaty null and void.

The British did not enforce Articles No. 3 and 5, and Capt. Gordon exacted his tribute with a light touch.

One Alexandria cracker baker saw the invaders empty his cellars of a good many barrels of flour without favoring him with any payment. But he acknowledged, in telling of his experiences, that "they performed the exploit in as civil a manner as could well be supposed; for when he went on board to represent that something by way of a fair exchange would sweeten his recollections of the transaction very materially, the officers insisted on his sitting down and drinking wine with them to promote their better acquaintance. After thus oiling the hinges of friendship, they dismissed him with many smooth words and good-natured recommendations to think no more about the flour."

And an enterprising American midshipman, Capt. Napier relates, thinking it would be fine fun to carry off a British officer, "dashed into the town on horseback and, meeting no officers in the streets, came boldly down to the boats and seized a midshipman by the collar. The fellow was strong and attempted to get him on his horse. The youngster, quite astonished, kicked and squalled most lustily and, after dragging him a hundred yards, the American was obliged to drop his brother officer.

"This operation, which was lightning, created a considerable alarm. The men retreated to the boats, prepared their carronades, expecting every moment to be attacked by the cavalry, and were with some difficulty prevented from firing. This occurrence soon found its way to the mayor who came off in great alarm for the town. Capt. Gordon, with great good humor, admitted his apology and treated it as a midshipman's spree."

Taking twenty-one prizes, which he "weighed, caulked, and masted," Capt. Gordon reports loading "from 15,000 to 18,000 barrels of flour, 800 hogsheads of tobacco, 150 bales of cotton, with a quantity of sugar and other commodities . . . by the 31st of August." At which date Ross's army had long since evacuated Washington.

Contrary winds delaying his departure, Capt. Gordon had bad news from Captain Henry L. Baker, who sailed 18-gun brig *Fairy* upriver from anxious Adm. Cochrane: the Americans had begun building batteries to harass the British fleet's downriver retreat.

Navy Secretary Jones and Commodore John Rodgers, who with his own hand on flagship *President* had fired the war's first shot, set the plan. And with upwards of 1,000 marines, including some of Barney's flotillamen eager for another fight, Com. Rodgers went about disputing Capt. Gordon's passage by means of two batteries and fire ships.

The first battery, under Captain David Porter who had captured the first British vessel in the war and gone on to fame in frigate *Essex*, went up at the "White House," below Mount Vernon on the Virginia shore. The second battery, under Commodore Oliver Hazard Perry of Lake Erie's great fleet victory, went up at Indian Head, some 10 miles below the White House battery, on the Maryland shore. Com. Rodgers himself improvised the fire ships at the Washington Navy Yard, and brought them down to Alexandria to attack the British squadron from the rear.

What with foul winds, frequent grounding on shoals, and the need to protect twenty-one sailing prizes, Capt. Gordon had his hands full. He met Capt. Porter first.

Fighting with three 18-pounders under a white flag blazoned with "Free Trade and Sailors' Rights," Capt. Porter had the counsel of the indomitable James Monroe, just appointed in place of Gen. Armstrong as Secretary of War and in command of the Tenth Military District. He also had the support of General John P. Hungerford's regiment of Virginia

militia, which included a company of riflemen, and of Brigadier-General Robert Young's Alexandria militiamen and volunteers who had not seen action at Bladensburg. Capt. Porter's
battery gave Capt. Gordon's squadron a bad four days.

On 2 September Capt. Gordon's bomb, *Meteor*, a gunboat,
a mortar boat, and brig *Fairy*—standing out of battery range
—opened with shells. To fire effectively on *Meteor*, Capt.
Porter moved one of his 18-pounders a mile to an advance
point. The bombardment continued all day . . . with no other
effect, Capt. Porter informed the Navy Secretary, "than to ac-
custom the militia to the danger."

Bomb *Devastation* having previously grounded, Capt.
Gordon had had to anchor his squadron a few miles above
Fort Washington. This gave Com. Rodgers an opportunity to
ignite his fire ships and send them downstream toward the
British. Wind failed, however, and Capt. Gordon's small
boats towed the American fire ships away and chased the
commodore's barges back up the Potomac.

On 3 September, Capt. Gordon sent bomb *Aetna* and
rocket-ship *Erebus* to help against Capt. Porter's battery. All
that day and succeeding night the British kept up a brisk fire
of shot, shells, and rockets.

Hoping soon to get long 32-pounders from Washington,
Capt. Porter made do with his 18-pounders and five 4- and
6-pounders of the Alexandrian artillery under Captain George
Griffith, and built a furnace for hot shot. His garrison took
Capt. Gordon's pounding for the whole of 4 and 5 September,
naval gunners and militia artillerists cutting up Capt. Gordon's
rocket ship. And when some 32-pounders and two mortars
arrived—without carriages but with ammunition—Capt.
Porter equipped two barges and hoped "that we should speedily be put in a proper state for annoying the enemy."

On 4 September Com. Rodgers had sent four barges and a
lighter in a night attack on *Devastation*, still trying to warp
off a shoal. But boats under *Fairy*'s Capt. Baker forced the
Americans ashore and at 11 P.M.—failing to dislodge them

after twenty minutes—withdrew, leaving nine Americans wounded.

The American barges went out again next morning, and Com. Rodgers set another fire ship adrift, but "the enemy was not harmed and his boats forced the barges to retreat." *Devastation* having got clear of the shoal, Com. Rodgers' rearguard action ended.

On the morning of 6 September, the enemy showed a disposition to move and Capt. Porter prepared to meet them with hot shot—overmatched against two frigates, a brig, three bombs, a rocket ship, and armed ships' boats. His infantry support fighting without intrenchments, he asked Gen. Hungerford to take a position in woods on the heights, but resourceful Capt. Gordon reached them by listing his ships to elevate his guns.

After an hour and a quarter, *Sea Horse* and *Euryalus* dropped down, anchored without musket shot of the battery, and poured their fired into the makeshift fort. The British bombs, following the frigates, discharged their mortars— loaded with musket balls—into the battery and neighboring woods. And *Fairy* convoyed the prizes outside the fighting vessels. The American loss: twelve killed, several wounded.

Capt. Porter's cannon fire and the Virginians' rifle fire from the water's edge did much damage on the enemy's decks, and Capt. Napier took a ball in his neck.

"It was quite impossible," he declared, "to dislodge the numerous body of sharpshooters who were under cover of the trees and did considerable execution through the ports . . . but their efforts were useless."

Capt. Porter's battery finally silenced, their prizes safely past, the British frigates slipped their cables and dropped downstream.

"We calculated all was over for that day," Capt. Napier reported. "We were mistaken. The *Fairy* and prizes were observed to anchor suddenly a few miles further down, having discovered fresh batteries."

The British had come on the second American battery, on Maryland's Indian Head. Here Com. Perry had the support of Bladensburg troops still smarting from orders to pull back when they had just begun to fight—under Maj. Peter and Capts. Burch, Stull, Davidson—with 6-pounders which they used "in the handsomest manner." For an hour this battery kept up a destructive fire on *Erebus*, which grounded in attempting to pass.

"From fourteen to eighteen guns were mounted in this new position, and a considerable interruption was expected," Capt. Napier chronicles. But "in the morning we weighed, the *Sea Horse* leading and the *Euryalus* bringing up the rear, and were agreeably surprised at being able to pass quietly. We ascertained afterwards that the batteries were hardly finished, and the powder and shot had been expended the night before." Com. Perry had one man wounded.

Cochrane's anxiously waiting fleet had pushed into the Potomac to bring Capt. Gordon out if necessary, going up and down "by night as well as by day without pilots, each taking care of the others as the colliers do in going up the Swin." But Capt. Gordon reached Chesapeake Bay 9 September with no further harassment, his Alexandrian cruise having lasted twenty-three days.

"The hammocks were only down twice; each ship was ashore at least twenty times." His total loss: seven killed, thirty-five wounded.

Peter Parker, captain, frigate *Menelaus*, gone with several smaller vessels to divert the Americans above Baltimore while Ross and Capt. Gordon pointed for Washington, did not fare so well.

At the little village of Moorfields on Maryland's Eastern Shore, in the moonlight of 30 August, he landed for "one more frolic with the Yankees" before rejoining Cochrane's fleet. That morning, according to an officer who dined with him alone, he had lost his gold-laced cocked hat overboard. He said, very thoughtfully and in a very unusual manner, "My head will follow this evening."

Capt. Parker's marauding party of 260 set out to capture 170 men of Lieutenant-Colonel Philip Reed's Twenty-first Regiment, encamped half a mile from the beach. In a sustained fight at Caulk's Field, the British wounded three Americans slightly, killing none.

But Capt. Parker left nine dead on the field; and nine wounded, six of whom died in the next few hours. Hit by buckshot, he too died—before his men could carry him to his barges. Preserved in a hogshead of Jamaica rum, gallant Peter Parker's body went back to England, for a poetical eulogy by his cousin Lord Byron and burial in London.

6

JAMES MADISON had served in the Constitutional Congress and, at 63, remembered the vicissitudes of the Revolution. Distressed but not dispirited, he returned to Washington 27 August to take up quarters in the French Ambassador's rented Octagon House with the First Lady. During each of the past four days he had spent from fifteen to twenty hours on horseback.

Following the Bladensburg debacle, original plans had called for him to join Navy Secretary Jones at Charles Carroll's Bellevue home in Georgetown. There, Jones had Dolly Madison under his aegis, along with his own family, the Carroll family, and navy clerk Edward Duvall, nephew of the supreme court justice.

But the President found roads clogged with defeated troops and sent Tench Ringgold with a message to the Jones entourage to meet him and his party—which included Rush, Gen. Mason, Charles Carroll, and servants—at Wiley's tavern on the Difficult Run stream near Great Falls, in Virginia; he would cross the Potomac into Maryland via Conn's ferry and rejoin the army.

The legend of the Madison hegira from Washington has the President cowering in a hovel and the First Lady excoriated by her husband's political enemies as both suffered the drenching indignities of stormy weather—a sleazy fabrication of cloudy recollections and malicious reporting. The facts confute the legend.

The night that saw the President's House go up in flames found James Madison at the Salona (Virginia) home of the Reverend John Maffitt, only one mile from where Dolly Madison and the Jones caravan stayed at the Rokeby home of Richard Hendry Love. On the second day, 25 August, the Madisons met at Wiley's tavern where the First Lady remained until her return to Washington.

A small, thin man of five feet six, James Madison ordinarily looked reserved, forbidding, even sour; but he combined a fiery spirit with gentle gaiety. Meeting this perennially black-garbed man with his old-fashioned hair style (a large club highly powdered, locks without curl or frizzing, hair combed down on his forehead), foreign diplomats expressed surprise "to find in the conversation of the great statesman, of the wise administrator, as much of sprightliness as of strength."

When he could throw off the cares of state, at home over dinner, his pale face shone as he "set his table guests into roars of laughter over his stories and whimsical way of telling them." His blue eyes "sparkled like stars under his bushy grey eyebrows"; a look of mischief "used to lurk in their corners." Close friends found him easy, familiar, plain—and "virtuous and enlightened."

To his servant Jennings he was "one of the best men that ever lived," never in a passion, taking only one glass of wine with his hearty midday meal, and "an excellent judge of horses." While President he never had less than seven in his Washington stables.

His inherited strong character, his mind trained at a vigorous preparatory school and Princeton, made it imperative for Madison to deal with men whose understanding matched his own. To abandon the capital to redcoated physical force because of Armstrong's lack of military foresight and Winder's lack of military talent galled.

At midnight of that second day in exile from Washington, the President, Secretaries Rush and Jones, Gen. Mason, chief clerk John Graham, and dragoon guards went to Conn's ferry. Jones returned to the wives and children at the tavern; the other men crossed over the Potomac into Maryland next morning, 26 August, and rode to Montgomery Court House in their over-all objective of making contact with Winder and the army. They arrived at 6 P.M.; Winder and his soldiers had departed at noon for Baltimore.

After following for some 6 miles, the presidential party stayed the night at the Brookeville home of Quaker Caleb Bentley where Col. Monroe and others kept the President abreast of the British retreat. He rode into Washington next day, 27 August, at 5 P.M.

The President met a wave of indignation against the Secretary of War's indolence in defending the District by suggesting to Gen. Armstrong that he leave the city and, on 30 August from Baltimore, Gen. Armstrong sent his resignation. Madison gave the War Department post, along with command of the Tenth Military District, to Monroe who, at Montgomery Court House, had helped Winder reassemble the militia for a march to support Baltimore, which loomed as the next British point of attack. When New York's Governor Daniel D. Thompkins declined his offer of the State Department, the President continued Monroe in that Cabinet post too.

Picking up the pieces in the aftermath of Ross's rout of the militia at Bladensburg, the sack of the capital, and Capt. Gordon's seizure of Alexandria, Washington's ire waxed as its panic waned. A fighting fervor took hold, fanned by "highest eulogiums" for the militia's spirit and accomplishment in the White House and Indian Head encounters with Capt. Gordon's squadron.

"They fought their 6-pounders until their ammunition was expended, and coolly retired with their guns, when ordered to do so, under a shower of the enemy's shot," praised Capt. Porter. "The militia who came under my immediate notice and were attached to my command, voluntarily or otherwise, conducted themselves in a manner which reflects on them and their country the highest honor. Many, before the battle, requested to be posted near me, and there was no instance where one offered to retire until I gave the order to retire."

Obviously the nation in 1814 lacked none of the fighting qualities that had distinguished it in the Revolution, as *The Enquirer* of Richmond pointed out two days after Ross and Cockburn had departed from the capital:

> For the benefit of our citizens let it also be recollected that when Philadelphia, then the seat of our government, then a large and populous town, was taken by the enemy during the war of the Revolution, it struck no terror into the American soil. No man looked down. No man cowered. The war ended gloriously; for it procured us the greatest boon which could be worn by a brave people.
>
> Who then desponds? The power of the State is in motion. The man who is at the head of it is an energetic officer—who deserves and who possesses our confidence.

Publisher Niles in his *Register* expressed the new feeling, at Baltimore:

> The Spirit of the Nation is roused. If the barbarian warfare of an inflated enemy would not have roused it, our liberties had perished forever. War is a new business with us, but we must "teach our fingers to fight" and Wellington's invincibles shall be beaten by the sons of those who fought at Saratoga and Yorktown. We can more easily become a military nation than any in the world, and we must become one or be slaves.

In New York, Mayor DeWitt Clinton, who had opposed the war, spoke out:

"The questions are not now whether the war was just

or unjust in its commencement; whether the declaration of it was politic or expedient; whether its causes have long ago ceased or not; whether our government might or might not have brought it to a speedy termination; or whether they have done their duty towards us since they involved us in this war. These are solemn questions which will one day be agitated, and which must be answered hereafter.

"The present inquiry is: Will we defend our country, our city, our property, and our families? Will we go forth to meet and repel the enemy?"

In Boston, Newport, and Philadelphia men organized and equipped themselves for armed service.

England, which received initial news of Washington's capture with exultation, read succeeding details with shame.

Said the *London Statesman:*

> Willingly we would throw a veil of oblivion over our transaction.

The *Liverpool Mercury* prophetically pointed out:

> . . . if the people of the United States retain any portion of that spirit with which they successfully contended for their independence, the effect of those flames will not easily be extinguished.

Ross and Cockburn had ravaged Washington "deliberately under definite instructions, as an act of retaliation." This became crystal clear with Monroe's receipt 31 August of a letter from Cochrane, dated 18 August but not sent from the flagship until 29 August:

> Having been called upon by the Governor General of the Canadas to aid him in carrying into effect measures of retaliation against the inhabitants of the United States for the wanton destruction committed by their army in Upper Canada, it has become imperiously my duty, conformably with the nature of the Governor General's application, to issue to the naval force under my command an order to destroy and lay waste such towns and districts upon the coast as may be found assailable.

Objective British historian C. P. Lucas shines a revealing light on the controversy which raged immediately and later over this retaliation.

For the real ground upon which both the expediency and the justice of destroying Washington's public buildings could be defended, he observes, "we must go back again to the Chancellor of the Exchequer's words, and his reminder of the burning of York: 'Be it remembered that York was the capital of Upper Canada. Although a small town it was a capital.'

"York might be a tiny capital, the British settlers in Upper Canada might be few in number, it might be expedient to be generous and forbearing in dealings with the United States in order to cultivate their good graces for the time to come; but whether the burning of the Washington buildings was right or wrong, whether it was politic or whether it was not, Lord Liverpool's government, in taking the responsibility for it, consciously or unconsciously, acted on a sound, wholesome, and not ungenerous instinct that the wrongs of the colonies should be requited upon the wrongdoers not less but more than if they had been directly inflicted upon the motherland herself."

Sir James Mackintosh, British authority on international law, epitomized the effect of the Ross–Cockburn vandalism: "It was an enterprise which most exasperated a people, and least weakened a government, of any recorded in the annals of war."

6

BANNER OVER BALTIMORE: 11 SEPTEMBER 1814

I

THE BRITISH INVADERS, too, faced a problem of union—chiefly that of getting the high command together on what move to make next.

While waiting for Ross and Cockburn to rejoin him from the Washington expedition which had gone ahead against his expressed order, Cochrane decided against another such deep inland thrust with attendant anxieties. Baltimore loomed a likely prize, and on 28 August he wrote Bathurst to send out 4,000 more troops and marines immediately.

"Baltimore may be destroyed or laid under severe contribution," he advised the British War Secretary, "but our present force is not adequate to the attempt without incurring more risk than it would be prudent to do."

Meanwhile he would take the fleet to Rhode Island and quarter his force on the country there until November. As he elaborated in a 2 September letter, his plan would indicate a possible British attack on New York and thus keep American troops too busy to go to the Canadian border. When his reinforcements arrived, he would return to the Chesapeake where "the worst army we have to contend with is the climate."

Reports on the British troops back from the American capital bore Cochrane out. American heat had killed as many men as had American muskets. American storms had scared more soldiers than had American cannon. And American water plagued them with diarrheas. The troops had no quarrel with American fish and game, however, and for ten days recuperated off the Patuxent and the Potomac on a diet of Chesapeake Bay crab, turtle, rockfish, rabbit, and turkey.

While their men recovered from the Washington march, Cochrane, Cockburn, Ross and their staffs chose up sides on whether to attack Baltimore. With the Washington invasion a successful *fait accompli*, Cochrane apparently forgot Cockburn's disobedience of orders and, smelling glory, now looked optimistically on British chances for taking Baltimore without the 4,000 additional troops.

Cockburn declared against moving out of the Chesapeake to Rhode Island, urging prompt descent on Baltimore; Deputy Quartermaster-General DeLacy Evans lined up with the admiral. Ross opposed an attack on Baltimore; Harry Smith lined up with the general.

As Harry Smith describes the fateful meeting:

"Sir Alexander Cochrane, Admiral Cockburn, and Evans, burning with ambition, had urged General Ross to move on Baltimore. The General was against it, and kindly asked my opinion. I opposed it, not by opinions or argument, but by a simple statement of facts.

"1. We have, by a ruse, induced the enemy to concentrate all his means at Baltimore.

"2. A *coup de main* like the conflagration of Washington may be effected once during a war, but can rarely be repeated.

"3. The approach to Baltimore Harbour will be effectually obstructed.

" 'Oh,' says the General, 'so the admirals say; but they say that in one hour they would open the passage.'

"I laughed. 'It is easier said than done, you will see, General.' (The passage defied their exertions when tested.)

"4. Your whole army is a handful of men, and the half of them are sick from dysentery.

"5. Your success in the attack on Washington is extraordinary, and will have a general effect. Your success on Baltimore would add little to that effect, admitting you were successful, which I again repeat I doubt, while a reverse before Baltimore would restore the Americans' confidence in their own power and wipe away the stain of their previous discomfiture.

"General Ross says, 'I agree with you. Such is my decided opinion.' "

A few days later Cochrane sent Harry Smith home with official reports on the Washington invasion.

"The day we were to sail in the *Iphigenia*," Harry Smith reveals, "as I left the *Tonnant*, kind-hearted General Ross, whom I loved as a brother, accompanied me to the gangway. His most sensible and amiable wife was at Bath. I promised to go there the moment I had delivered my dispatches, and of course I was charged with a variety of messages. In the warmth of a generous heart he shook my hand and said:

" 'A pleasant voyage, dear Smith, and thank you heartily for all your exertions and the assistance you have afforded me. I can ill spare you.'

"My answer was: 'Dear Friend, I will soon be back to you, and may I assure Lord Bathurst you will not attempt Baltimore?'

" 'You may.' "

With his reports off for England, Cochrane moved the fleet from the Patuxent down to Tangier Island and, on 6 September, Cockburn sailed off in *Albion* for Bermuda. But before he reached the capes, he had a signal to turn back.

Cochrane and Ross had changed their minds—the combined fleet would attack Baltimore!

"The approaching equinoctial moon," Cochrane explained, rendered it "unsafe to proceed immediately out of the Chesapeake."

He would not go to Rhode Island to await arrival of the asked-for 4,000 troops, as previously suggested. Instead he would occupy the intermediate time to advantage in a "demonstration on the City of Baltimore, which might be converted into an attack should circumstances appear to justify it."

Behind a number of the fleet's lighter vessels, Cochrane, Cockburn, and Ross on 10 September sailed for the Patapsco River, with some difficulties.

"The labour of getting up to Baltimore without pilots, feeling our way with the lead, whilst boats on each bow and one ahead were sounding also, gave little time for respite," Midshipman Lovell confesses. "The heat of the weather too was very great, the thermometer varying only from 79° to 82° in the shade during most of our severest services, which added much to the exhaustion."

Capt. Codrington, adverse critic of the new invasion, watched activities closely, "surprised that so sensible a man as General Ross should be led away by the opposite opinions . . . heroism will do wonders certainly, and there is that still to look to, but I believe there is too much on hand even for that, and I wish the job were well over."

2

BALTIMORE defended itself against Indians in 1752 with a stockade which 200 neighbors put up with their own hands and axes.

In 1814 neighbors again turned out, 50,000 strong, in common defense against another "red savages" invasion. Wielding picks, shovels, and wheelbarrows, they dug intrenchments and threw up batteries across a city grown to America's third largest, fourth wealthiest.

Unlike dilatory Washington, Baltimore started girding up

its military loins as far back as November 1811 when the Maryland Legislature passed acts requiring all white male citizens between 18 and 45 years to come to the aid of the country. With civil officers, educators, physicians, ferrymen, pilots, coastal sailors, and conscientious objectors exempted, the city's militia mustered, drilled, camped in three brigades of about 3,000 men each.

Drafted and volunteer, these militiamen had sprung to their arms when Cockburn came up to the head of the Bay in 1813, responding to such notices as this from Captain John H. Rogers of the Fifty-first Regiment:

Sir,
In obedience to a Regimental Order, you will furnish yourself with a Knapsack, Canteen, and Ten rounds ball Cartridges, suitable to your Firelock, and hold yourself in readiness to repair immediately to my quarters on the George Town Road, with arms and accoutrements, upon any Alarm that may be given, by the ringing of the watch bell. Our Enemy is at the door, therefore it is hoped that no Man, who wishes well to his Country, will be missing.

And while young blades like John Pendleton Kennedy paraded gay uniforms before admiring femininity, Baltimore's solid citizens put up solid defense dollars. When their first money advances to the federal government showed no signs of returning in the form of civic protection, the City Council appropriated $20,000, followed by $500,000, to do for themselves.

Under the knowing eye of a Revolutionary War soldier who held a sword voted him by the Continental Congress—sixty-two-year-old Major-General Samuel Smith, U. S. Senator from Maryland and head of a large and prosperous Baltimore shipping firm—officers of the United States Army and Navy helped strengthen and add to the city's defenses.

Gen. Smith carried out a major task. He had first to protect Baltimore from frontal water assault via the Patapsco

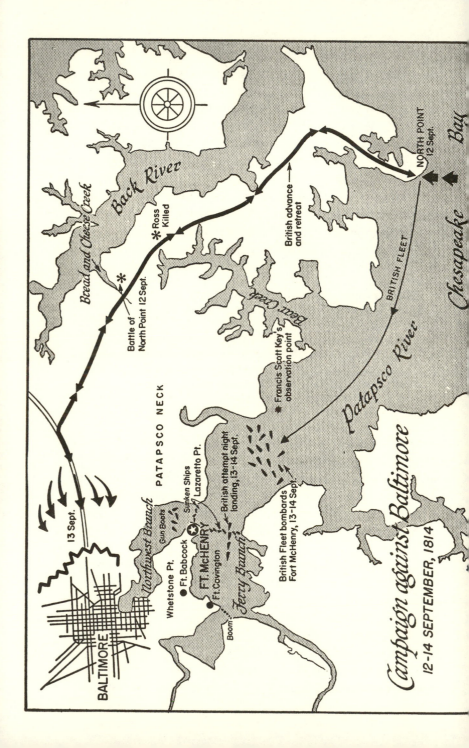

Campaign against Baltimore
12-14 SEPTEMBER, 1814

Chesapeake Bay

NORTH POINT
12 Sept.

BRITISH FLEET

British advance
and retreat

Patapsco River

Francis Scott Key's
observation point

Bear Creek

British Fleet bombards
Fort McHenry, 13-14 Sept.

British attempt night
landing, 13-14 Sept.

Lazaretto Pt.

Sunken Ships

Gun Boats

Whetstone Pt.

FT. McHENRY

Ft. Babcock

Ft. Covington

Boom

Ferry Branch

Northwest Branch

PATAPSCO NECK

Back River

Bread and Cheese Creek

Ross Killed

Battle of
North Point 12 Sept.

13 Sept.

BALTIMORE

which divided at Whetstone Point into a northern and a southern arm—the North West Branch extending 2½ miles to the very center of the city, the Ferry Branch swinging around within a mile of it.

Where the river forked at Whetstone Point, Gen. Smith repaired the earthen ramparts of Fort McHenry's outer batteries and replaced defective gun platforms and carriages. He emplaced 42-pounders from the wrecked French frigate *L'Eole*, and installed furnaces for heating shot. To protect the fort's rear, he erected two small works on the Ferry Branch —Forts Covington and Babcock. And he set up a small battery at the Lazaretto point, across from Fort McHenry, to help protect the North West Branch entrance.

Gen. Smith also had to prepare for a land attack. The enemy could put troops ashore at North Point, on the bay, march them 5 miles in a northwesterly direction along narrow Patapsco Neck which stretched between the Patapsco and the Back River, and come on Baltimore from the east. When British invasion loomed inevitable, Gen. Smith tackled that part of the city's defense program with the help of every citizen not subject to military service.

A Committee of Vigilance and Safety acted for Baltimore's civilian defense. Comprising three representatives from each of the city's eight wards and from adjoining Eastern and Western Precincts, its thirty members included at least sixteen merchants, a judge, a cabinetmaker, a brickmaker, a butcher, a boatbuilder, and a sea captain.

Voted into office the day Ross and Cockburn burned Washington, the committee at once divided all nonmilitary males into four labor districts, to work for a day in rotation on the earthworks along the city's eastern hills. Free Negroes joined in; masters sent their slaves. Visitors from out of town were invited to take part, and the anxious parents of Gen. Smith's twelve-year-old nephew found their lost boy in the mile-long intrenchments—shoveling.

In due time "strong Batteries with their heavy Guns in

great number, stood with gaping mouths, watching for our enemy on our Eastern Heights," one citizen tells us. "The Enemy far or near, we neither relaxed our exertions nor our Ardor. Martial law was proclaimed; we were mustered into the Service of the U. S."

Baltimore turned into a camp, its citizens into soldiers. A subcommittee studied care of the wounded; volunteer women rolled bandages.

On 3 September Navy Secretary Jones ordered Com. Rodgers from Alexandria to Baltimore to help in its defense and to animate his fellow citizens who, Jones wrote, "rely with perfect confidence upon the efficiency of your force and upon your individual influence, skill, and industry."

Com. Perry and Capt. Porter joined him immediately after Capt. Gordon's fleet battled past their Potomac batteries. On 6 September, the *Intelligencer* in Washington reported:

> Fourteen wagons-full of our noble seamen, the first surmounted with the well-known standard of "Free Trade and Sailors' Right," the whole preceded by the Hero of Valparaiso and cheered by their boatswain's whistle, passed through this city on their way to Baltimore Tuesday evening.

Com. Rodgers worked along with the vigilance committee, with Gen. Smith, and with Major George Armistead of the U. S. Artillery, in command of Fort McHenry. He blocked the river where it divided at the fork, sinking twenty-four schooners, brigs, and ships across the North West and the Ferry Branches. He stationed a fleet of twelve small one-gun boats in the North West Branch, with 360 men under Lieut. Rutter. Under Lieut. Frazier, he sent seamen and marines—out of sloop-of-war *Erie* and frigates *Java* and *Guerriere*, just built in Baltimore and Philadelphia—to the supporting shoreline batteries which Gen. Smith had set up earlier.

With the situation in hand on the waterfront, Com. Rodgers took some 200 gunners up on the range of hills that rose from the north edge of the inner harbor, roughly in line with Fort McHenry and extending northward parallel with the city's eastern limits. On these elevations, together called Hampstead Hill, Gen. Smith's defensive earthworks, trenches, and bastions embraced 100 guns on field carriages. Here, Lieutenant Thomas Gamble commanding, the naval gunners awaited the British land attack in "Rodgers' Bastion."

Along with Maryland's county troops, militia marched to Baltimore from Pennsylvania, Delaware, and Virginia—a local soldier reports: "well officered, of good material & well equipped, quartered in Tents, Ropewalks & along the Eastern Hills stretching to Harford Avenue."

To this man in the ranks, the prospect looked pleasing. "Our numbers, our strong & well manned Batteries occupying the very best possible positions, inspired us with confidence that we would prove more than a Match for the British Veterans, which could be brought into action under these disadvantageous Circumstances."

But what the united citizens of Baltimore had put together for defense of their city, the disunity of leadership threatened. The problem: who would command Baltimore's defenders— Gen. Smith or Gen. Winder?

Samuel Smith commanded the 3rd Division of Maryland militia, with headquarters in Baltimore. He held the rank of major-general.

William Winder commanded (under Monroe) the Tenth Military District, which included Baltimore. He held the lower rank of brigadier-general.

Winder marched toward Baltimore the morning of 26 August with his reassembled Bladensburg troops. En route he met an express from Smith. As a major-general, said Smith, he had assumed command.

In the ensuing legalistic controversy, Winder asked his uncle—Maryland's Governor Levin Winder—whether he confirmed Smith's claim; Uncle returned a cryptic reply. Appeals to Monroe, War Secretary by now and for all practical purposes superseding Winder as commander of the Tenth District, ended with a lengthy and diplomatic—but friendly—summation in which Monroe pointed out that a remedy for the situation might require Congressional intervention.

On 10 September, Monroe notified Winder:

"The force at Baltimore being relied on for the protection of that place, Annapolis and all other places in this District on the Bay, being under General Smith, the movement of troops must be under his control." Monroe expressed full confidence "that you will do everything in your power to promote the success of our arms in defense of our Country."

And in an enclosed copy of a letter to Smith, Monroe nailed the lid down:

"Gen. Winder, who as Commander of the District has made calls for the militia from different quarters, is instructed to cooperate and give you all the aid in his power."

Good soldier and patriot, Baltimore lawyer Winder smothered his feelings.

Man of action, Smith went about the city on horseback seeing to the field work. In his major-general's cocked hat with high white plume and his blue coat faced with buff in the Revolutionary tradition—blue ribbon and eagle of the Cincinnati hanging from left lapel to show he had fought in Washington's army—he animated his fellow citizens "to buckle on their arms and prepare to defend their homes and all that was dear to free men." Some few had suggested capitulating.

About noon, Sunday 11 September, news of the impending British attack spread over Baltimore. Three alarm guns sounded from the courthouse green, churches dismissed their congregations, citizens assembled, and the militia stood to arms under Gen. Smith ready to fight the Chesapeake's invaders.

At almost the same moment, at Plattsburg on America's northern border, a thirty-two-year-old veteran of America's naval wars against France and the Barbary pirates and a thirty-two-year-old West Pointer administered to another invading British force a crushing defeat whose echoes would ring long in history. Commodore Thomas Macdonough had captured an entire fleet on Lake Champlain, and Brigadier-General Alexander Macomb, with 1,500 citizen soldiers from New York and Vermont, had sent 15,000 of Wellington's seasoned redcoats scampering back to Canada.

To check a British landing at North Point—where Chesapeake Bay met the Patapsco—American forces marched out of Baltimore along the hot and dusty Philadelphia road about 3 P.M. led by Brigadier-General John Stricker, another Revolutionary War veteran, 55.

Gen. Stricker's troops comprised the Fifth, Sixth, Twenty-seventh, Thirty-ninth, and Fifty-first Baltimore Regiments, with riflemen, cavalry, and artillery; they included also one volunteer Maryland company from Hagerstown and one company each of volunteers from York, Hanover, and Marietta in Pennsylvania. Some went forth in blue militia coats and pantaloons, with white vests; some wore civilian clothes, with high hats. They totaled 3,185.

By 8 P.M. the brigade had marched down Long Log Lane on the North Point peninsula to strategic ground near a Methodist meeting house. Here, halfway from Baltimore to North Point, Gen. Stricker halted. Sending his cavalry forward 3 miles to Gorsuch's farm and posting riflemen near a blacksmith's shop 2 miles ahead of the cavalry to prevent the British coming up by surprise, he encamped his troops for the night.

3

BRITAIN'S INVASION FORCE sailed on Baltimore under a heavy press of canvas, happy to see that "utmost consternation prevailed in every town or village opposite to which we made our appearance."

In passing Annapolis, Lieut. Gleig reveals, the fleet "stood in so close as to discern the inhabitants flying from their houses: carts and waggons loaded with furniture hurrying along the road, and horsemen galloping along the shore as if watching the fearful moment when the boats should be hoisted out and the troops quit the vessels. Wherever a lighthouse or signal station was erected, alarm guns were fired and beacons lighted."

This picture of panic that the British expected to find also in Baltimore stimulated the confident flotilla as, on 11 September, it came in sight of the projecting headland where Ross planned to disembark the troops—North Point.

"The distance from the point to Baltimore did not exceed fourteen or fifteen miles, a space which might easily be traversed in a day," Lieut. Gleig optimistically estimated.

As at Benedict, the bustle of preparation filled troopships and transports.

"Three days' provisions were cooked, as before, and given to the men," Lieut. Gleig chronicles. "And as we were now to carry everything by a *coup-de-main*, twenty rounds of ammunition were added to the sixty with which soldiers are usually loaded. A blanket, with a spare shirt and pair of shoes, was considered enough for each man on an expedition of so rapid a nature; while brushes and other articles of that description were divided between comrades, one carrying what would suffice for both. Thus the additional load of twenty cartridges was more than counterbalanced by the clothing and necessities left behind."

Because dusk fell before the fleet reached anchorage, Ross attempted no immediate landing. Orders went out to have boats ready at dawn. Every man would sleep in his clothes. The stir and noise of getting ready, with the subsequent calmness and stillness of expectation, gave Lieut. Gleig food for thought. He did not expect the troops to obtain possession of a place so important as Baltimore without fighting.

"This arming and this bustle seemed, in fact, to be the prelude to a battle. But no man of the smallest reflection," he philosophized, "can look forward to the chance of a sudden and violent death without experiencing sensations very different from those which he experiences under any other circumstances. When the battle has fairly begun, I may say with truth, the feelings of those engaged are delightful; because they are, in fact, so many gamblers playing for the highest stake that can be offered.

"On the other hand, the warlike appearance of everything about you, the careless faces and rude jokes of the private soldiers, and something within yourself which I can compare to nothing more seemly than the mirth which criminals are said sometimes to experience and to express previous to their execution—all these combined to give you a degree of false hilarity, I had almost said painful, from its very excess. It is an agitation of the nerves such as we may suppose madmen feel; which you are inclined to wish removed, though you are not unwilling to admit that it is agreeable."

He looked around him. The heat of the day had departed . . . a full clear moon shone bright in a cloudless sky . . . he distinctly saw the shore, less than 2 miles distant . . . and tide murmured "like the gushing of a mountain stream" around the ships moored near by. Voices of sentinels as they relieved one another on deck and the occasional splash of oars as a boat rowed to the admiral's ship for orders sounded musical in the quiet night.

But the night's calm quickly passed. At 3 A.M. ships began to lower boats. Watchmen roused soldiers from their sleep.

The same precautions which had formerly covered the landing again were adopted, Lieut. Gleig records, "several gun-brigs laying themselves within cable's length of the beach and the leading boats in every division being armed with carronades, loaded and ready for action. But as had been the case at St. Benedict's, they were unnecessary, for the troops reached shore without opposition and leisurely formed in an open field close to the river.

"It was seven o'clock before the whole army was disembarked and in order for marching."

Bomb vessels, brigs, and frigates pushed farther upriver in

their part of the amphibious attack. Three frigates went aground abreast of Capt. Codrington's *Surprise*, "hauling themselves over the banks into deep water by main strength."

Sizing up the naval situation, Capt. Codrington observed:

"What the army may find on the land side, I know not; but on this side the enemy is so well prepared for defence by nature and by art that we can do little either towards capturing or destroying the town."

He added:

"I do not like to contemplate scenes of blood and destruction. But my heart is deeply interested in the coercion of these Baltimore heroes, who are perhaps the most inveterate against us of all the Yankees."

Ross and Cockburn went ashore on North Point on the morning of 12 September with the British light brigade, six fieldpieces and two howitzers drawn by horses, the second brigade, sailors, marines, armed Negroes, and the third brigade —a force of some 4,000.

At the end of an hour, Ross halted his stretched-out column and went a quarter of a mile to the left of the road with Cockburn and six other officers for breakfast at the farm of Robert Gorsuch. Forced to furnish the meal, this descendant of the first Englishman to settle the region in 1660 also had to serve the redcoats as royal taster, drinking and eating something of every dish he provided.

While the British officers breakfasted, American outposts got word back to Gen. Stricker.

"Insulted at the idea of a small marauding party thus daringly provoking chastisement," Stricker reported to Gen. Smith, "several of my officers volunteered . . . to punish the insolence of the enemy's advance; or, if his main body appeared, to give evidence of my desire for a general engagement."

Asked, as he left the Gorsuch farm with Cockburn, where he planned to go, Ross said:

"We are going to Baltimore."

Told he might find obstacles in his path, he responded:

"I will eat supper in Baltimore—or in hell."

Riding out on a white horse with Cockburn and his well-mounted staff in an advanced guard of about sixty men, Ross left the troops at some considerable distance, to Cockburn's discomfort. This, the admiral observed after they had ridden about 2 miles, seemed contrary to their former practices; they always had kept troops collected, flank companies spread into the woods.

When a British patrol brought up three prisoners, young Baltimore light horsemen who had separated from advanced skirmishers, the captives delivered Gen. Stricker's wish for a general engagement. And though Baltimore's defenders totaled only about 12,000, the prisoners added that—after meeting Gen. Stricker's force—Ross would find 20,000 more Americans waiting at the city's gates to fight his army.

Having encountered the Baltimore militia at Bladensburg, Ross confidently replied that he would take the city "if it rains militia."

While Ross closed ranks, Gen. Stricker's volunteer skirmish party of some 250 men and one 4-pounder opened a brisk fire. Amazed at American temerity in attacking, Ross rode forward to see what the skirmishers meant to do. Three young American militiamen—one of whom had climbed a tree to gather peaches—fired at him. He went down, tradition has it, under the musket ball and buckshot of Daniel Wells and Henry M. McComas.

Ross fell into the arms of his aide, Captain Duncan Mc-Dougall, whom Cockburn sent galloping back for Col. Brooke, second in the present army chain of command.

Due to the woods, the main body of British troops had not witnessed the calamity. So that when Capt. McDougall reached them, riding at full speed "with horror and dismay on his countenance and calling loudly for a surgeon," as Lieut.

Gleig describes, "every man felt within himself that all was not right, though none was willing to believe the whispers of his own terror.

"But what at first we would not guess at, because we dreaded it so much, was soon realized. The aide-de-camp had scarcely passed when the General's horse, without its rider, and with the saddle and housing stained with blood, came plunging onwards. Nor was much time given for fearful surmise as to the extent of our misfortune.

"In a few moments we reached the ground where the skirmishing had taken place and beheld General Ross laid by the side of the road, under a canopy of blankets, and apparently in the agonies of death. . . . All eyes turned upon him as we passed and a sort of involuntary groan ran from rank to rank, from the front to the rear of the column."

Col. Arthur Brooke took over. "An officer of decided personal courage," Lieut. Gleig concedes, "but, perhaps, better calculated to lead a battalion than to guide an army. . . .

"Under him we continued to march on, sorrowful indeed but not dejected. The skirmishing had now ceased, for the American riflemen were driven in, and in a few minutes we found ourselves opposite to a considerable force drawn up with some skill and occupying a strong position. Judging from appearance, I should say that the corps now opposed to us amounted to six or seven thousand men."

These "six or seven thousand" Americans comprised Gen. Stricker's North Point battle formation of some 2,275.

4

ON RECEIVING NEWS of the British landing, Gen. Stricker, at 7 A.M., had sent back his baggage with a strong guard and formed a line at the head of Long Log Lane—across the mile-wide peninsula—with his right resting on Bear Creek, an arm of the Patapsco, and his left extending toward Bread and Cheese Creek, an arm of the Back River.

The Fifth Regiment held the right from creek to main North Point Road, the Twenty-seventh held the left from road to creek, and the artillery of six 4-pounders lay posted directly at the head of the lane in the interval between the Fifth and the Twenty-seventh.

Three hundred yards behind this front, Gen. Stricker formed a second line with the Thirty-ninth Regiment on the left and the Fifty-first on the right. For reserve, he threw the Sixth back to a position half a mile behind the second line.

The Fifth and Twenty-seventh would, he ordered, receive the enemy. If necessary, they would fall back through the second line and re-form on the right of the reserve Sixth Regiment.

Gen. Stricker sent riflemen to the skirts of a thick pine wood, beyond the blacksmith's shop, with a large sedge field in front. Taking advantage of this cover, they would annoy the enemy's advance when the American scouting cavalry brought back word of the British approach.

Gen. Stricker's well-laid plans went quickly awry.

As scouts announced rapid enemy progress up the main road, "I flattered myself with the hope that the riflemen would soon proclaim, by a galling fire, their still nearer approach," Gen. Stricker told Smith. "Imagine my chagrin when I perceived the whole of the rifle corps falling back upon my main position, having too credulously listened to groundless information that the enemy were landing on Back River to cut them off."

His hopes of early annoyance to the enemy being thus frustrated, Gen. Stricker threw the riflemen on the right flank of his front line, with a few additional cavalry, and secured that flank. The volunteer party, which had gone out to annoy Ross and Cockburn's advance, returned—after considerable skirmishing had shown that its cavalry and artillery could not provide enough support on disadvantageous ground to harass the British approach.

At about 2:30 P.M. the enemy opened fire with rockets.

Seemingly harmless as they crossed Gen. Stricker's left flank, the screeching missiles prepared the line for the sound of its own artillery. The American guns soon opened up, and for some minutes cannonading continued brisk between the American 4-pounders and the British 6-pounders and howitzers —until Gen. Stricker ordered his guns to wait for the enemy to come within close canister range.

At this point of the British attack, obviously directed against the American line's left where Bread and Cheese Creek looked fordable, Gen. Stricker's strategy again fell short as the inexperience of unseasoned militia in field maneuvering under fire took an upper hand over patriotic fervor.

Gen. Stricker moved to strengthen his left. He brought the Thirty-ninth forward into the front line, next to the Twenty-seventh, with two pieces of artillery on its own left. To make this flank still more secure, he ordered the Fifty-first to cross from its second-line position on the opposite side of the lane and line up at right angle to the Thirty-ninth's left, so that the Fifty-first's volleys would sweep the inlet if the enemy's attack developed.

Badly executed, the order created confusion that took frenetic brigade action to correct.

As Gen. Stricker watched, the enemy's right column advanced. And the Fifty-first, "unmindful of my object to use its fire in protection of my left flank in case an attempt should be made to turn it, totally forgetful to the honor of the brigade, and regardless of its own reputation delivered one random fire and retreated precipitately, and in such confusion as to render every effort of mine to rally them ineffective."

They stampeded!

As at Bladensburg, the militiamen holding the line's left looked on this panic—and a few gave way. But firing became general along the entire American front of some 1,400—and the line held.

At 2:50 P.M., the British moved in for the kill. Having galloped along his line to check, Col. Brooke gave the order to charge and the signal "echoed back from every bugle in the army when, starting from the ground where they had lain, the troops moved on in a cool and orderly manner."

But, Lieut. Gleig confesses, "a dreadful discharge of grape and canister shot, of old locks, pieces of broken muskets, and everything which they could cram into their guns, was now sent forth from the whole of the enemy's artillery."

The British tasted the flavor of American militia resistance for upwards of an hour. On the American right, held by the Fifth, they advanced in column to suffer severe loss from musketry and canister, "for in that quarter it seemed to be the flower of the enemy's infantry, as well as the main body of their artillery."

The redcoats found the Twenty-seventh and Thirty-ninth equally formidable despite exposure of their left flank as a result of the Fifty-first's defection.

At 3:45 P.M., Gen. Stricker decided his citizen soldiers had accomplished as much as they could against a greatly superior force. They had made an impressive stand. New to warfare, the militiamen had shown coolness and valor against veterans. Gen. Stricker ordered them back to the reserve regiment, which stood well posted to receive them, and they retired— for the most part, Gen. Stricker felt, well.

The exhausted British did not pursue.

But the fatigued state of his retiring men and the possibility of a quick enemy attempt to turn his right flank, caused Gen. Stricker to fall back along the Philadelphia road to Worthington's mill. With his troops in good order to meet the British when they came closer to the city, Gen. Stricker encamped here—on the left of Smith's entrenchments and half a mile in advance of them.

Col. Brooke—the day being far gone and his men done in "as is always the case on the first march after disembarkation" —halted for the night "on the ground of which the enemy had been dispossessed." This ground, which Gen. Stricker had used to harass and delay the enemy, cost the British 39 killed, 251 wounded, and a considerable number deserted, including two of Ross's body servants.

But, elated over having pushed the Americans back in his first battle as commanding general, Col. Brooke let his imagination run when he reported to Earl Bathurst:

"The enemy lost in this short but brilliant affair [he estimated it took him only fifteen minutes; Lieut. Gleig figured two hours from start to finish] from 500 to 600 killed and wounded; while at the most moderate computation, he is at least 1,000 *hors de combat*. The Fifth Regiment of militia, in particular, has been represented as nearly annihilated."

The "annihilated" Fifth lost 80 men out of 550 in 12 September's delaying action at North Point. Col. Brooke's representations sugared off to: 24 Americans killed, 139 wounded, 500 taken prisoner—with 1 American gun in British hands.

5

THE BRITISH had a fresh taste of nature's American elements next day, Tuesday 13 September.

At an early hour, Lieut. Gleig reports, "the troops were roused from their lairs and, forming upon the ground, waited until daylight should appear. A heavy rain had come on about midnight, and now fell with so much violence that some precautions were necessary in order to prevent the fire-locks from being rendered useless by wet.

"Such of the men as were fortunate enough to possess leathern cases wrapped them around the locks of their muskets; the rest held them in the best manner they could, under their elbows, no man thinking of himself, but only how he could best keep his arms in a serviceable condition.

"As soon as the first glimmering of dawn could be discerned, we moved to the road and took up our wonted order of march. But before we pushed forward the troops were desired to lighten themselves still further by throwing off their blankets, which were to be left under a slender guard until their return. This was accordingly done and, being now unencumbered except by a knapsack now almost empty, every man felt his spirits heightened in proportion to the diminution of his load."

But the British made slow going of it because "the Americans had at last adopted an expedient which, if carried to its proper length, might have entirely stopped our progress," Lieut. Gleig declares. "In most of the woods they had felled trees and thrown them across the road. As these abattis were without defenders, we experienced no other inconvenience than what arose from loss of time, being obliged to halt on all such occasions till the pioneers had removed the obstacle. So great, however, was even this hindrance, that we did not come in sight of the main army of the Americans till evening, although the distance travelled could not exceed ten miles.

"It now appeared that the corps which we had beaten yesterday was only a detachment, and not a large one, from the force collected for the defense of Baltimore."

A rude shock on so wet a day!

During the morning, Col. Brooke had tried to get at Baltimore from the north, the left of the city's defense line. But Smith had sent Winder's troops there the night before to support Gen. Stricker's North Point forces.

Skillfully opposed in his flank maneuver, Col. Brooke concentrated in front of Baltimore's defenders between 1 and 2 P.M. And pushing forward to within a mile of the American intrenchments, he drove in Smith's videttes with obvious intention of staging an evening attack.

Smith waited for this with considerable confidence. In his trenches and batteries he had Gen. Stansbury's 11th Brigade from Baltimore County, Brigadier-General Thomas M. Foreman's 1st Brigade from Harford and Cecil Counties, Captain George Stiles's Baltimore artillery, Colonel John Findlay's and Colonel Cobean's Pennsylvania volunteers, and Com. Rodgers' seamen and marines—"all prepared to meet the enemy."

Reconnoitering with Cockburn, Col. Brooke faced what he judged to be an army of 20,000 men, with 100 cannons on heights covered by breastworks, with a strong fort toward the river on its right, and with a chain of field redoubts covering its left and commanding the entire ascent to Baltimore.

"It would be absurd," Lieut. Gleig concedes, "to suppose that the sight of preparations so warlike did not in some degree dampen the ardour of our leaders."

Accordingly, Col. Brooke halted his army, let his sodden foot soldiers light cooking fires as best they could in the torrential rain, and sent a messenger to Cochrane asking naval support for the stalled land probe of the British amphibious attack on Baltimore.

Cochrane received Col. Brooke's request for a diversion on the waterfront after a long day of trying to provide such a diversion. Since sunrise British warships had battered Fort McHenry on Whetstone Point with bombs and rockets.

6

IN 1776, local Revolutionary War patriots reported to Maryland's Council of Safety that their "fort at Whetstone is ready to mount eight guns" to deter British cruisers in the Chesapeake from molesting Baltimore.

In 1794, the state turned to the federal government, and Washington appropriated $4,225.44 for a 20-gun battery and small redoubt, sending military engineer J. J. Ulrich Rivardi to study the problem of permanent harbor defense on Whetstone Point. Over the years, succeeding improvements—paid for in part by popular subscription and erected in part by voluntary citizen labor—transformed the Whetstone redoubt into a French-style, five pointed star-shaped "fortification of mason work, with batteries, magazines, and barracks" named Fort McHenry.

The fort's name honored Irish-born James McHenry, Revolutionary War surgeon, Baltimore citizen, Maryland representative to the Constitutional Congress, and Secretary of War under John Adams. As War Department head, McHenry in 1799 sent a second lieutenant's commission to nineteen-year-old George Armistead. And on Tuesday 13 September 1814 *Major* Armistead commanded at Fort McHenry.

In Philadelphia this same day, on the eve of returning to France after many years of American political asylum, one of the fort's builders—Colonel John Foncier—tagged a touching note onto a good-by letter to James McHenry:

> P.S.—It is a painful idea to me that the beautiful city of Baltimore be exposed to the disasters of War; but my mind will be a little solaced if Fort McHenry does answer the purpose for which it was established, and affords me the Satisfaction of having contributed to your defence.

From the center of Fort McHenry, a high staff flew a 42 x 30-foot flag which a Baltimore committee that included Com. Barney, Gen. Stricker, and Lieutenant-Colonel William McDonald of the Sixth Regiment had commissioned from Mrs. Mary Young Pickersgill.

A designer of ships' colors and pennants, Widow Pickersgill, in her small home, had cut eight broad red stripes, seven broad white stripes, a large blue square, and fifteen big white stars for the huge flag and, with the help of fourteen-year-old daughter Caroline and/or two nieces, laid them out and sewed them together on a nearby brewery floor at a cost of $405.90 for labor and 400 yards of bunting.

Smith and his soldiers on the city's hills could see the flag; so could Cochrane and his gunners, from their ships.

Under the big flag, in two waterfront batteries before the fort and in the fort's bastions, Maj. Armistead had: U. S.

Artillery under Captain Frederick Evans and U. S. Infantry under Lieutenant-Colonel William Steuart and Major Samuel Lane; Sea Fencibles under Captains M. S. Bunbury and William H. Addison; volunteer Baltimore artillery captained by John Berry, Charles Pennington, and Judge Joseph H. Nicholson; and a detachment of Barney's flotillamen under Lieutenant Samuel Rodman—about 1,000 effectives.

They had 12-pounders, 18-pounders, and 42-pounders— one of which, from the days of the Revolution, bore the seal of King George III.

Weeks of preparing Fort McHenry's defenses had worn Maj. Armistead down to the point of exhaustion, and Cochrane's opening salvos added frustration to fatigue. For when five British bomb vessels (*Aetna, Devastation, Meteor, Terror, Volcano*) saw that their shells reached the fort, they anchored two miles off, with rocket-ship *Erebus*. And when Maj. Armistead opened his batteries in a brisk fire from guns and mortars at the enemy, he found that:

"Unfortunately our shot and shell all fell considerably short of him . . . a most distressing circumstance, as it left us exposed to a constant and tremendous shower of shells, without the remote possibility of our doing him the slightest injury."

During the morning Fort McHenry's defenders did little but watch shells pass overhead.

At 2 P.M., however, one hit the southwest bastion—killing a man, wounding several, and dismounting a 24-pounder cannon. This created renewed fleet action.

"The bustle necessarily produced in removing the wounded and remounting the gun," Maj. Armistead reported, "probably induced the enemy to suspect that we were in a state of confusion, as he brought in three of his bomb ships to what I believed to be good striking distance.

"I immediately ordered a fire to be opened, which was obeyed with alacrity through the whole garrison, and in half an hour those intruders again sheltered themselves, by with-drawing beyond our reach."

A single British bomb, a cast-iron sphere of 13-inch di-ameter and 1½-inch-thick walls, weighed some 190 pounds with bursting powder charge of 9 pounds. Ignited through a wood fuse packed with finely mealed powder, this bomb left the ship from a muzzle-loading mortar that weighed more than 8,000 pounds. Elevated to 45 degrees, the mortar could hurl the bomb 2.38 miles, after which it "destroys the most substantial buildings by its weight and, bursting asunder, creates the greatest disorder and mischief by its splinters."

British bomb-ship *Aetna,* attacking Fort McHenry, had massive timbers and powerful reinforcing beams to carry mortars on her 102-foot-long deck. And since she and her sister vessels sent hundreds of bombs to land inside the fort's walls, Fort McHenry's defenders survived partly because the bombs, somewhat like British rockets, did not always explode.

By dusk of that day, Britain's naval thrust, too, had stalled.

But the invading ships continued to hurl shells and rockets at Fort McHenry, and the cooking fires of British soldiers continued to burn ominously at the edge of the besieged city's entrenchments. Baltimore greeted the dark of 13 September with appreciable misgiving. What would the night bring?

7

PARTICULARLY CONCERNED with Fort McHenry's fate, since he fervently believed his country's destiny depended on how Baltimore's citizen soldiers measured up to this British attack by land and by sea, Francis Scott Key kept an uneasy vigil on a small American dispatch boat* that lay out beyond the en-emy's bomb vessels. As he watched the flag over the fort, he had cause to worry; he had taken part in the battle of Bladens-

* See Notes, Chap. VI.

burg and had seen American spirit wither under similar rocket fire.

Key had arrived at his fateful observation post by a long chain of events. He had started out wanting no part of Mr. Madison's War. A Georgetown lawyer, 33, who once had considered going into the ministry . . . a supporter of widespread social work . . . a man generous with money and emotion for friends and strangers . . . a sensitive and serious poet . . . he opposed war. A patriot, he joined the Georgetown field artillery company of Maj. Peter. He saw the British invade from Benedict. Aide to Gen. Walter Smith, he witnessed the debacle at Bladensburg.

After the British return to their fleet from Washington, Key had a call from his brother-in-law, Richard E. West, who owned the Wood Yard estate. West came to Georgetown to tell about his family physician, sixty-five-year-old William Beanes. As Key knew, Ross had used the Beanes home in Upper Marlboro for British headquarters on the march to Washington.

From his brother-in-law Key learned that Dr. Beanes—together with former Maryland Governor Robert Bowie and an Upper Marlboro resident named John Rodgers—had worked out a plan to keep local roads free of straggling British soldiers and had directed the capture and jailing of six. Whereupon British marines burst in on Dr. Beanes at 1 A.M. 27 August, rousted him and two overnight guests out of bed, and galloped them to the fleet where Ross clapped them into the brig.

Learning details, Ross released Dr. Beanes's two guests, but held the physician under threat of a Bermuda or Halifax trial—most likely for treason, based on a spurious charge that he had been born in Scotland. After Ross—and Cochrane and Cockburn—ignored a petition from Prince Georges County residents for the doctor's release, Richard West appealed to his brother-in-law, and Key went to the President.

Unwilling to condone a British policy of making civilians prisoners-of-war, Madison gave Key his blessing and sent him to Gen. Mason, American commissioner of prisoners. With a letter from Gen. Mason to Colonel John Stuart Skinner, Baltimore lawyer active in effecting prisoner exchanges, Key left Washington the night of 2 September.

With great foresight, he stopped at two hospitals caring for British wounded—Capitol Hill and Bladensburg—and offered to take letters to the fleet, in one of which letters a sergeant detailed the unusually good medical care that the Americans gave him.

Key and Col. Skinner went on board an American cartel vessel in the upper Chesapeake and scoured the bay for the British flotilla which, on 7 September, they found near the mouth of the Potomac.

Cochrane, Ross, and Cockburn welcomed the pair on board flagship *Tonnant*, and dined them. When, however, the British officers learned that the Americans wanted Dr. Beanes, Cochrane quickly cooled, Cockburn expressed anger, and Ross refused to change his mind—until he read Sergeant Hutchinson's letter.

"Dr. Beanes deserves more punishment than he has received," Ross finally declared. "But I feel myself bound to make a return for the kindness which has been shown to my wounded officers—and upon that ground, and that only, I release him."

But Ross kept Dr. Beanes, along with Key and Col. Skinner, under guard to prevent a leak of British plans to attack Baltimore.

And because *Tonnant*, overcrowded with military personnel, had no space for visitors, he sent the three Americans on board frigate *Surprise*, captained by Cochrane's son Thomas. When, on reaching Baltimore, *Tonnant* could not ascend the shallow Patapsco River after Ross went ashore to his death on North Point, Cochrane carried his flag over to *Surprise* in order to command the bombardment of Fort McHenry—and shifted the Americans back on board their own cartel vessel, still under marine guard.

Thus, behind the advanced British line of bomb-ketches, Francis Scott Key and Dr. William Beanes and Col. John Stuart Skinner on 13 September watched the enemy attack Fort McHenry.

"I saw the flag of my country," said Key later, "waving over a city—the strength and pride of my native State—a city devoted to plunder and desolation by its assailants. I witnessed the preparations for its assaults, and I saw the array of its enemies as they advanced to the attack. I heard the sound of battle; the noise of the conflict fell upon my listening ear, and told me that 'the brave and the free' had met the invaders."

As a wet and gloomy twilight drew down on Fort McHenry, Dr. Beanes kept asking keener-sighted Key if the flag still flew. Until dark, Key replied that it did; after that, he could only hope.

Holding the fort, George Armistead—sick, frustrated by British out-of-range tactics, hiding a knowledge of vulnerable powder magazines—kept his men underground as much as possible. His batteries, alert for possible small-boat assault, fired an occasional shell.

Holding Hampstead Hill, Samuel Smith and the city waited for Col. Brooke to storm their heights.

The night continued dark, wet, and cold.

In Fort Babcock's six-gun battery where Sailing Master John A. Webster guarded the Ferry Branch on Fort McHenry's right, rain drove down over exposed gunners, who shivered numbly. Webster saw his reserves crouching for shelter beneath the low parapets, "drawing their clothing closer around their chilled bodies, while the lurid glare from the bursting bombs revealed momentary glimpses of the enemy's fleet, standing in bold relief against the dark, somber background."

Twenty-seven years old, six feet two and powerful, Webster had served with Com. Barney in *Rossie*, in a Chesapeake flotilla barge, and at Bladensburg. He had seventy-five men for his six guns, and he had kept them busy on the exposed battery for four days. Anxious to take part in the fighting, he and his men began to sense action about 11 P.M. when British bombing became brisk.

Webster suspected a serious project. He increased lookouts. He had his guns' charges withdrawn and the entire battery reloaded—double-shotted with 18-pound balls and grapeshot.

Close to midnight, he heard a splash of oars and the sound of muffled sweeps. Unable in the dark to distinguish objects twenty feet away, he mustered his men at the guns. When he discovered dim lights moving in different quarters, apparently no more than 100 yards above him—next to Fort Covington—he opened fire.

The first discharge found marks. Webster heard the balls from his guns smash into attacking barges. Shrieks and cries filled the night. The sound of rowing ceased.

While Webster's gunners kept a "perpetual circle of brilliant flame" around their battery, guns from Fort Covington, from Fort McHenry's barbette, from Lazaretto Point, and from the gunboats guarding the basin joined the American defensive barrage.

Under Capt. Napier, 1,250 British assaulted the waterfront. They attacked in twenty-two barges and a schooner which they brought into position with sweeps.

They came under cover of dark, but their rockets whooshed overhead to light the shore, and muzzle blasts of the 12-pounders, 18-pounders, and 24-pounders on their barges set up targets for American gunners to shoot at through the dark.

In the city, houses shook on their foundations under the heavy naval give-and-take. On the American cartel-ship's deck, Key watched every shell from the moment it was fired until it fell, listening with breathless interest to hear if an explosion followed.

"While the bombardment continued," he reports, "it was sufficient proof that the fort had not surrendered."

Capt. Napier's assault lasted two hours. His flotilla tried to reach shore with scaling ladders, to storm Fort Covington, and thus to assail Fort McHenry and Baltimore from the rear. But Lieutenant Henry S. Newcomb and his naval gunners held at Fort Covington.

At 1 A.M., his right shoulder broken by a handspike, Sailing Master Webster noted a movement among the British barges.

"Suddenly three [signal] rockets ascended from their midst, the colored lights flashing and scintillating on high, followed by an immediate retreat on the part of the attacking force down the river . . . acknowledgement on the part of the British that they were beaten and had failed in their plans."

At sundown, Cochrane had sent word to Col. Brooke:

"You are on no account to attack the enemy, unless positively certain of success."

As before Bladensburg, Cockburn insisted the army go into action despite Cochrane's orders.

To discuss the chances of success, however, Col. Brooke called a council-of-war—which Cockburn refused to attend. And while Capt. Napier tried to effect his landing on the waterfront, the army huddle continued.

Col. Brooke and staff reasoned that without the fleet's help any plan of attack would bring losses to outweigh even complete success . . . lacking ship transport to carry off booty, for instance, they could not pay survivors for their toil and console them for loss of comrades.

"We should only fight to give us an opportunity of re-enacting the scenes of Washington," Lieut. Gleig confesses. "If an attack failed, it was hardly possible to avoid destruction."

When Capt. Napier's water assault foundered, Cochrane sent further word to Col. Brooke, advising him to move his troops back to the transports. The council leaped at the admiral's advice.

Leaving bright campfires behind to deceive the entrenched city, Col. Brooke—like Capt. Napier, frustrated by unexpectedly stubborn American resistance—withdrew his troops from Baltimore's gates.

Cockburn's reactions went unrecorded.

Lieut. Gleig reports that, as of 3 A.M. 14 September 1814, "the rain, which had continued with little interruption since the night before, now ceased, and the moon shone out bright and clear. We marched along, therefore, not in the same spirits as if we had been advancing, but feeling no debasement at having thus relinquished an enterprise so much beyond our strength."

8

AT DAWN of that Wednesday, with British shells still bursting in the air, Key strained anxious eyes toward Fort McHenry and saw America's flag over the fort—to him, after that long night, a star-spangled banner even though holed by one bombshell and torn by several pieces of another.

"My heart spoke," Key told friends. "Even though it had been a hanging matter to make a song, I must have written it."

In twenty-five hours of continuous bombardment, with two slight intermissions, Cochrane's bomb and rocket vessels had hurled not less that 150 tons of metal at Fort McHenry ... "from 1,500 to 1,800 shells," Maj. Armistead calculated.

"A few of these fell short," he reported. "A large portion burst over us, throwing their fragments among us, and threatening destructions. Many passed over, and about 400 fell in the works."

The American loss at Fort McHenry: 4 dead, 24 wounded, 2 buildings materially injured; the powder magazine did not blow up.

While enemy bomb-ketches ceased firing and retreated to their more distant frigates at 7 A.M., Key made notes for his song on the back of a letter. After Cochrane freed him and his companions, he worked on his lines in the boat that rowed him to shore. He enlarged on the verses at the Fountain Inn on Light Street, near Orange Alley. At patriotic pitch, he finished the verses during the night.

Next morning, 15 September, he showed his finished song to his brother-in-law, Capt. Nicholson, whose artillery company had helped keep Fort McHenry safe. The enthusiastic judge had a fourteen-year-old printer's apprentice named Samuel Sands set type for the song that day in Benjamin Edes's newspaper shop.

"Defence of Fort McHenry" circulated through exultant Baltimore in handbill form. Set to the popular English drinking tune Key had heard in American camps at Wood Yard and Old Field—"To Anacreon in Heaven"—it reached Colonel MacConkey's tavern next to the Holliday Street Theater.

Here Ferdinand Durang—eighteen-year-old actor who had left the touring company of his father John (America's first great impresario) in York to volunteer in the Pennsylvania militia and, with his brother Charles, defend Baltimore—sang America's national anthem for its first time in public. The city rejoiced.

Halting Col. Brooke's troops at the city's gates and Cochrane's warships in the river, Baltimore had given the enemy's invasion attack two death blows. The redcoats, withdrawing, declared that "the capture of the town would not have been a sufficient equivalent to the loss which might probably be sustained in storming the heights."

Key said it differently:

"Thus be it ever when freemen shall stand. . . ."

Although Smith sent Winder in pursuit of Col. Brooke's army, Winder's fatigued men did not seriously molest the British retreat and, on 15 September, Col. Brooke re-embarked his troops at North Point, "carrying with me about two hundred prisoners, being persons of the best families in the city."

Lieut. Gleig described the Baltimore aftermath:

"No one talked of a future enterprise, nor was the slightest rumor circulated as to the next point of attack. The death of General Ross seemed to have discouraged the whole plan of proceedings and the fleet and army rested idle like a watch without its mainspring."

Spirited American resistance and competent military defense had crushed British overconfidence. Baltimore had shown the Chesapeake countryside—and the nation—what a firm stand could achieve. The military warned against relaxation, however, and citizen soldiers held themselves ready to move again at a moment's warning.

But aggressive British action faded out in the next months. Cochrane left the Chesapeake 19 September, having arranged for exchange of prisoners. In October, Cockburn went to Bermuda to revictual and refit. Capt. Barrie of *Dragon* watched over troopships and transports in the bay. Following the Cockburn pattern, Capt. Barrie undertook to continue harassing the shore.

"Come," he used to say; "we have not had a shooting party this some time. I have just had information that a body of Yankee militia, with a fieldpiece or two, are in such a place —we must go and take it from them."

With too much sense to raid the same village twice, Capt. Barrie saw to it that American militia along the Chesapeake stayed alert. He also kept the bay's packet-boat captains on their toes to elude capture and loss of foodstuffs to British sailors and marines whom Capt. Barrie had to put on half rations.

Cockburn rejoined the squadron from Bermuda. And on 18 December 1814 the marauding admiral led the last of Britain's warships out of Chesapeake Bay with its cold American weather, its heavy American gales, and its inhospitable American militia.

7

PEACE AT GHENT:
24 DECEMBER 1814

Wʜᴇɴ ᴛʜᴇ *Baltimore Patriot* resumed publication 20
September, it concluded its first editorial after the city's gallant exertions with:

> . . . how nobly is the fame of our country rescued! How
> is the flame which was burst forth at *Lexington*, and
> blazed in perfect brightness at *Yorktown*, rekindled!

When the Thirteenth Congress met in its third session in
Blodget's Hotel, Washington's *National Intelligencer* observed:

> . . . there can now happily be no rational opposition to
> the course of the government. . . . On the main question
> of resistance or submission to Britain, there cannot be a
> dissentient voice.

Hailed with delight throughout the nation, Baltimore's
defense restored the young country's pride. Coming almost
simultaneously with her overwhelming victory at Plattsburg,
it also reverberated in the halls of Ghent's *Hotel des Pays-Bas.*

On 8 August in the old Flemish capital, a channel crossing from London, British peace commissioners had offered conqueror's demands to stunned American ministers. Elderly, taciturn Lord Gambier and obscure admiralty lawyer Dr. William Adams had let thirty-year-old Under Secretary for War and the Colonies Henry Goulburn rattle off peace terms that included no slightest relief from British impressment on the high seas.

With considerable Yankee resource, the Americans had started bargaining from weakness: titular commission head John Quincy Adams (not even a cousin of his British counterpart at the meeting), Delaware Senator James Asheton Bayard, former Speaker of the House Henry Clay, astute Albert Gallatin, and United States Minister to Sweden Jonathan Russell.

The night Washington burned, America's commissioners had presented Britain's messenger boys (the government had not deigned to send Bathurst himself) an eclectic note which John Quincy Adams felt sure would "bring negotiations very shortly to a close."

But Britain had come back again with arrogant demands that included a slice of Maine, and the apparently futile bargaining went on.

The break came 17 October with news from America that Gen. Smith had ended Adm. Cochrane's invasion hopes in front of Hampstead Hill and Com. Macdonough had scuttled Gov. Prevost's on Lake Champlain.

Goulburn wrote Bathurst, 21 October:

> If we had either burnt Baltimore or held Plattsburg, I believe we should have had peace on the terms you sent to us, in a month at latest. As things appear to be going on in America, the result of our negotiations may be very different.

When Wellington told Britain's Cabinet that even he could do his country "but little good" by going to fight the Americans on their home soil, Bathurst from London saw the handwriting on the wall of the *Hotel des Pays-Bas* in Ghent.

At 6 P.M. Saturday 24 December 1814—Christmas Eve—
at the British *Chartreux*, a former monastery in which
Napoleon had honeymooned, Britain's commissioners attested
with America's to a "Treaty of Peace and Amity between his
Britannic Majesty and the United States of America."

The Ghent accord did not even allude to the matter of
free trade (freedom to do business with whomever America
chose, without British hindrance) or sailors' rights (to the
same protection on sea as granted citizens on land)—the immense reputation which American seamen had earned during
the war guaranteed those points more effectively than a
treaty.

The treaty served as an armistice: American hotheads who
cried that it settled nothing cooled off, the English no longer
whisked sailors off American ships, and respect for neutral
rights rose among nations. In effect, the treaty restored the
status quo: and gave the former belligerents an opportunity
(which both seized) to reconcile their original differences
through joint commissions whose adult handling of territorial
claims developed a close and permanent mutual respect.

Militarily, the War of 1812 record showed a series of
American defeats (many of them disgraceful) on land, with a
few remarkable victories as at Baltimore, Plattsburg, and
(after the peace, yet revealing the national morale through
the militia's achievements) at New Orleans.

At sea, each side captured or destroyed some 1,700 merchant vessels; the United States profiting more, since the
larger British bottoms averaged more valuable cargoes.
America's fighting ships wrote brilliant pages in history's
naval annals.

The military record also showed:

1. That the United States could not successfully invade
   Canada,
2. That Great Britain could not successfully occupy
   America, and

3. That retaliation ends in emptiness.

To learn this over two-and-a-half years cost the United States:

1,500 men killed in land battles,

3,500 men wounded in land battles,

9,700 total land casualties, including prisoners-of-war,

30,000 casualties on land and sea, in camp and hospital,

A national debt rise of $17 million.

Politically, Britain's punitive operations in the Chesapeake had long-range effects.

William Cobbett anticipated them when London prematurely announced the fall of Baltimore:

> It has been stated in the newspapers that Admiral Cochrane has taken Baltimore. . . . Baltimore is hardly taken, and will, I dare say, never be taken without a most bloody contest. . . . But supposing it to be so, how are we to maintain that position? . . . and if we could maintain it for a year, how much nearer are we to our objective? . . . What is that place, or even all the state of Maryland, when we are talking of this great republic inhabited by free men resolved to defend their country?
>
> From the first it was allowed by me that we should do immense mischief; that we might burn many villages, towns, and cities, destroy mills and manufactories, and lay waste lands upon the coast to the great loss and distress of numerous individuals . . . but I anticipated that these acts would only tend to unite the Americans and, in the end, produce such a hatred against us as would not only render final success impossible, but as would tend to shut us out from all further connexion and intercourse with that great and fertile region.
>
> There seemed to be wanting just such a war as this to complete the separation of England from America; and to make the latter feel that she had no safety against the former but in the arms of her free citizens.

Appreciating that the country did indeed feel this way, President Madison sent to Congress a message on the peace that recommended a cutback of public expenses for military purposes, but admonished against a "sudden and general revocation of the measures produced by the war."

The war had shown America the need to put its Navy on a footing that would deter any nation from thoughts of attack; and which, through ensuing years of peace, would enable unharassed American sea commerce to replenish Europe's bare cupboards with American produce.

The war also had provided political perspective on the role of the citizen soldier. The nation had seen that volunteer militia trained as soldiers fought better than untrained civilians required to pick up arms and face an enemy. From Maj. Williams, who officially investigated the militia debacle at Bladensburg, came strong comment:

"Different persons will draw a different moral from the same story. The moral we are disposed to draw from the history of the battle of Bladensburg is not that Americans were too 'pusillanimous' to defend their seat of government and that, therefore, it would be safer to hire an army of foreign mercenaries to defend it for us; nor that militia troops are not to be depended upon and, therefore, a large standing army of regular troops is necessary; but that politicians of the fairest fame require watching, and will not hesitate to sacrifice or jeopard the interests and honor of their country in order to advance themselves or ruin a rival."

With Madison's early fears of growth of a military caste gone by the board, he asked Congress to provide:

—For the maintenance of an adequate regular force,

—For gradual advancement of the naval establishment,

—For improvement of harbor defense,

—"For adding discipline to the distinguished bravery of the militia and for cultivating the military art in its essential branches, under the liberal patronage of government."

Congress took steps. The militia's distinguished bravery so well proven in the determined and successful fighting of Baltimore's citizen soldiers—under experienced commanders and behind defensive works—put the country on a path which enabled it to face its next international crisis with regulars, supported by volunteers.

Europe came to see that America had both the spirit and the means of defense, and her government the ability to call them up.

The war showed that free government, slow to start moving, in motion acquires force that expands in proportion to its freedom—that "the union of these states is strengthened by every occasion that puts it to the test."

The spiritual results of the War of 1812 ranked second only to those of the Revolution which "segregated the materials for an independent nation"; the second war gave them new form and effective unity. Peace Commissioner Albert Gallatin who had kept a long and intimate watch on his country's development—as a representative in Congress, as personal advisor of two consecutive presidents, as Secretary of the Treasury—expressed it like this:

"Independent of the loss of lives and of the property of individuals, the war has laid the foundations of permanent taxes and military establishments which the Republicans had deemed unfavorable to the happiness and free institutions of the country. But under our former system we were becoming too selfish, too much attached exclusively to the acquisition of wealth; above all, too much confined in our political feelings to local and state objects.

"The war has renewed and reinstated the national feelings and character which the Revolution had given, and which were daily lessening. The people have now more general objects of attachment, with which their pride and political opinions are connected.

"They are more Americans; they feel and act more as a nation; and I hope that the permanency of the Union is thereby better secured."

James Madison appraised what his opponents once had

called Mr. Madison's War with the mature judgment of his years in the national service:

"If our first struggle was a war of our infancy, this last was that of our youth; and the issue of both, wisely improved, may long postpone if not forever prevent a necessity for exerting the strength of our manhood."

The country emerged from the War of 1812 proud and united.

At a Fourth of July celebration in America's once-burned Capitol, Francis Scott Key lifted high, for the world to see, the trophy which these United States had rewon in their Second War of Independence:

"My countrymen," he said, "we hold a rich deposit in trust for ourselves and for all our brethren of mankind. It is the fire of Liberty. If it becomes extinguished, our darkened land will cast a mournful shadow over the nations. If it lives, its blaze will enlighten and gladden the whole earth."

NOTES

When Great Britain invaded and captured Washington in 1814 some of the British soldiers and sailors who invaded and some of the American militiamen and seamen who resisted told what they did, saw, and felt. To convey the feeling that filled the United States at that time I have used these personal colorings in the hope of touching reality and approaching objectivity while relating the historical facts.

For their special contributions to an understanding of military leaders and actions on both sides, I am indebted to: British midshipmen Frederick Chamier who went on to become captain, and William Stanhope Lovell who made admiral; Subaltern George Robert Gleig who became chaplain-general of the British armies and when he died at 96 had over his Chelsea Hospital Chapel pulpit the American flag he captured at Bladensburg, and Brigade Major Harry Smith who ended as a lieutenant-general; American militiaman John Pendleton Kennedy who finally danced in the President's House—as Secretary of the Navy; Elbridge Gerry, Jr., gay young Washington blade; Paul Jennings, slave; John Adams Webster, sailing master with the same spirit that made his commodore—Joshua Barney—famous.

I am also indebted to: Charles Jared Ingersoll (who was there), B. J. Lossing (who came along soon afterwards), and Glenn Tucker (who researched prodigiously) for anecdotal material; Neil H. Swanson for references; John S. Williams for his great good sense in assessing the Washington investigation of what happened.

Acknowledgment for special material goes to the Department of the Army, the Department of the Navy, the Headquarters of the United States Marine Corps, and the Mariners Museum, as well as to the many libraries and historical societies consulted.

CHAPTER I

Political background: Butler, Hildreth, Hall, Holst.
Military: Daugherty, S. R. Brown, Perkins.
Color: Lossing, Marine, Wood.

CHAPTER II

American and British attitudes: Babcock, Brackenridge, Cobbett, Cockburn, Cullum, A. J. Dallas, P. M. Davis, James, Mahan, McMaster, O'Connor, Perkins, Roosevelt, Thomson, Wood.
Medical hazards: Ashburn, Mann.
Color and corroboration: Footner, Forester, Hall, Gerry, Lossing, Marine, Metcalfe, Niles, Paine, Tucker, Woodworth.

CHAPTER III

Background: American State Papers, Auchinleck, Babcock, Brannan, Brant, James, Lucas, Marine, Perkins, Robinson, Schouler, Wood, Woodworth.
Military: Fortescue, Gleig, Hadel, Mahan, Peck, Tunis, J. S. Williams.
Personalities: W. F. Adams, Bourchier, Brenton, Chamier, G. Dallas, Dundonald, Footner, Forester, Knox, Lovell, Paine, Soley.
Washington: Anthony, G. Brown, Clark, Duncan, Green, Gutheim, Holloway, Hurd, Moore, *National Intelligencer,* Some Unknown Foreigner, M. B. Smith, Tully.
Color and corroboration: Bowen, M. S. Davis, Gerry, Ingersoll, Lossing, Pratt, Tucker.

The United States sent York Parliament's mace back to Toronto 4 July 1934 as a gesture of mutual friendship.

Irving Brant spells Dorothy Payne Madison's popular first name Dolley and Glenn Tucker follows this style which appeared on early documents. It somehow seems more becoming to keep the Dolly which warm friends and devoted relatives so generally used.

Both Cochrane and Ross earned credit for passing disguised spies in and out of Washington at pleasure—one visiting Dolly Madison in woman's dress, another cadging food from Mrs. Suter—frequenting the taverns and hotels. American traitors acted as guides for the invasion march.

CHAPTER IV

Background: Armstrong, Brackenridge, Cullum, Gilleland, Ingraham, Marine, McLane, Perkins, Robinson, M. B. Smith, J. S. Williams.

Personalities: W. F. Adams, Bohner, Cresson, Gilman, Jenkins, Paine, Tuckerman.

Color and corroboration: Aldridge, An Officer of Gen. Smith's Staff, Beirne, Bourchier, M. S. Davis, Fay, Gleig, Hadel, Heightman, Ingersoll, Jennings, Lossing, Lovell, Peck, Rentfrow, Robinson, Harry Smith, Stahl, Swanson, Tucker, S. Williams.

CHAPTER V

Background: Aldridge, American State Papers, M. Davis, Hadel, Heitman, Ingersoll, Ingraham, Lucas, Marine, *Niles' Weekly Register*, Robinson, Roosevelt, The War, J. S. Williams.

Personalities: Anthony, Dean, Gay, Harry Smith, Jenkins, Napier, Paullin.

Washington: American Guide Series, G. Brown, Holloway, Hurd, Moore, Tully.

Color and corroboration: Duncan, Lossing, Park, Peck, M. B. Smith, Stuart, Tucker, Wallace.

CHAPTER VI

Background: Colston, Craighill, Cullum, Hadel, Hall, Hill, Hoyt, Fay, Fortescue, Marine, Perkins, Piper, Robinson, Roosevelt, Scharf, Sonneck, Spaulding, Thomson.

Individuals: Delaplaine, Durang, Paine, Paullin, Webster.

Color and corroboration: Bourchier, Brenton, A. S. K. Brown, Ingersoll, Lessem, Lossing, Lovell, Miller, Muller,

O'Connell, Preble, Semmes, Harry Smith, Stahl, Swanson, Tucker, Tunis, J. S. Williams, Woodworth.

In the *Baltimore Sun* of 5 January 1919 President James E. Hancock of the Society of the War of 1812 in Maryland, whose great-grandfather and grandfather saw the British fleet in the Patapsco, puts Key, Beanes, and Skinner on an American navy dispatch boat "of the old pilot boat construction." The story that Key saw the waving Star-Spangled Banner from Great Britain's *Minden* came into existence, Mr. Hancock points out, fifty years after the defense of Fort McHenry. At the time of the bombardment, according to the Admiralty, *Minden* sailed with the British East Indian squadron.

CHAPTER VII

Babcock, Brant, Butler, Cobbett, Cutler, Delaplaine, Engleman, Forester, Fortescue, Hadel, Ingersoll, Mahan, L. P. A. Paris, Perkins, Roosevelt, Tucker, J. S. Williams, Wood.

BIBLIOGRAPHY

MANUSCRIPTS AND OFFICIAL MATERIAL

Cockburn, George, "Queries from John Warren and Sidney Beckwith concerning defenses around Norfolk and the possibility of a successful amphibious attack by the combined forces of the British army and navy, with his answers." (June, 1813.) Manuscript in New York Public Library.

Durang, John, "John Durang's Memoir of His Life and Travels." (About 1816.) Manuscript held by Historical Society of York County.

Gerry, Elbridge, Jr., "Diary." Photostat of original diary, May–August, 1813, in New York Public Library.

Miller, Lewis, "Lewis Miller Chronicles." Manuscript held by Historical Society of York County.

McClellan, Edwin North, "History of the United States Marine Corps." Typescript held by Department of the Navy, Headquarters, U. S. Marine Corps.

Webster, John Adams, "Naval Yarns." Manuscript in Enoch Pratt Free Library, Baltimore, Md.

An Officer of Gen. Smith's Staff, "A Narrative of the Battle of Bladensburg; in a letter to Henry Banning, Esq." Held by Department of the Navy, Headquarters, U. S. Marine Corps.

No author, "History of Late War." (New York, 1832.) Held by Department of the Navy.

No author, "History of the American War of 1812." (Philadelphia, 1816.) Held by Department of the Navy.

MAGAZINES AND PUBLICATIONS

Admiralty Office, *Papers Relating to the War With America.* (House of Commons, 9 & 10 February, 1815.)

Aldridge, Frederick S., "Marines and Sailors Defend Washington." *Marine Corps Gazette* (March, 1950).

American State Papers, Gales and Seaton, Pubs. "Foreign Affairs," "Military Affairs," "Naval Affairs." (Washington, D. C.)

Bradford, J. Stricker, "Battle of Bladensburg." *Maryland Historical Magazine,* Vol. 5, No. 4 (1910).

Brown, Anne S. K., "Military Dress in Maryland." *Military Collector & Historian,* Vol. 7, No. 2.

Cockburn, George, "A Secret Letter to Admiral Cochrane." *Maryland Historical Magazine,* Vol. VI, No. 1 (1911).

Colston, Frederick M., "The Battle of North Point." *Maryland Historical Magazine,* Vol. II, No. 2 (1907).

Craighill, William P., "Baltimore and Its Defences, Past and Present." *Maryland Historical Magazine,* Vol. I, No. 1 (1906).

Davis, Madison, "An Almost Forgotten Battle." *Records of the Past,* Vol. 9, Pt. 4 (July/Aug., 1910).

Davis, Milton S., "The Capture of Washington." *U. S. Naval Institute Proceedings* (June, 1937).

Delaplaine, Edward S., "Gems of Francis Scott Key." (Leaflet, no date.)

Engelman, Fred L., "The Peace of Christmas Eve." *American Heritage* (December, 1960).

Foncier, John, "A Letter to James McHenry." *Maryland Historical Magazine,* Vol. V, No. 2 (1910).

Hadel, Albert Kimberley, "The Battle of Bladensburg." *Maryland Historical Magazine,* Vol. I, Nos. 2,3 (1906).

Hill, Richard S., "The Melody of 'The Star Spangled Banner' in the United States before 1820." *Offprint from Essays Honoring Lawrence C. Wroth, Library of Congress, 1951.*

Hoyt, William D., Jr., Ed., "Civilian Defense in Baltimore, 1814–1815." *Maryland Historical Magazine,* Vol. XXXIX, Nos. 3,4; Vol. XL, No. 1 (1944).

Lessem, Harold I., and Mackenzie, George C., "Fort McHenry —National Monument and Historic Shrine." *National Park Service Historical Handbook Series No. 5* (Washington, 1957).

McBarron, H. Charles, and Todd, Frederick P., "British 85th Regiment." *Military Collector and Historian* (Spring, 1955).

McLane, Allen, "Col. McLane's Visit to Washington, 1814." *Bulletin of the Historical Society of Pennsylvania*, Vol. I, No. 1 (March, 1845).

O'Connell, Frank A., "Story of the National Anthem, Fort McHenry and North Point." *National Star-Spangled Banner Centennial Programme* (Baltimore, 1914).

Piper, James, "Defence of Baltimore, 1814." *Maryland Historical Magazine*, Vol. VII, No. 4 (1912).

Rentfrow, Frank Hunt, "And to Keep Our Honor Clean." *The Leatherneck* (August, 1930).

Sanford, John L., "The Battle of North Point." *Maryland Historical Magazine*, Vol. XXIV, No. 4 (1929).

Semmes, Raphael, "Vignettes of Maryland History, from the Society's Collection of Broadsides." *Maryland Historical Magazine*, Vol. XL, No. 1 (1945).

Spaulding, Thomas Marshall, "The Battle of North Point." *The Sewanee Review* (Sept. 1, 1914).

Tyler, Samuel, "Memoir of Roger B. Taney." *Maryland Historical Magazine*, Vol. 282.

Woodworth, S., & Co. (Pub.), *The War: Being a Faithful Record.* (New York, Starting June 27, 1812.)

Robinson, Ralph, "Controversy Over the Command at Baltimore in the War of 1812." *Maryland Historical Magazine*, Vol. XXXIX, No. 3 (1944).

Robinson, Ralph, "New Light on Three Episodes of the British Invasion of Maryland in 1814." *Maryland Historical Magazine.* Vol. XXXVII, No. 3 (1942).

Robinson, Ralph, "The Use of Rockets by the British in the War of 1812." *Maryland Historical Magazine*, Vol. XL, No. 1 (1945).

BOOKS

Adams, Henry, *History of the United States During the Second Administration of James Madison*, Vol. II (New York, 1891).

Adams, William Frederick, Ed., *Commodore Joshua Barney.* (Springfield, Mass., 1912.)

Anthony, Katharine Susan, *Dolly Madison, Her Life and Times.* (Garden City, N. Y., 1949.)

Armstrong, John, *Notices of the War of 1812.* (New York, 1836.)

Ashburn, Percy Moreau, *History of the Medical Department of The United States Army.* (Boston, 1929.)

Auchinleck, Gilbert, *A History of the War Between Great Britain and the United States of America.* (Toronto, 1855.)

Babcock, Kendrick C., *The Rise of American Nationality.* (New York, 1906.)

Barney, Mary, Ed., *A Biographical Memoir of the Late Commodore Joshua Barney.* (Boston, 1832.)

Barrett, C. R. B., Ed., *The 85th King's Light Infantry.* (London, 1913.)

Beirne, Francis F., *The War of 1812.* (New York, 1949.)

Bourchier, J. B., *Memoir of Sir Edward Codrington.* (London, 1873.)

Brackenridge, Henry Marie, *The History of the Late War Between the United States and Great Britain.* (Baltimore, 1818.)

Brannan, John, Ed., *Official Letters of the Military and Naval Officers of the U. S. during the War of 1812.* (Washington, 1823.)

Brant, Irving, *James Madison: President.* (New York, 1956.)

———, *James Madison: Commander-in-Chief.* (New York, 1961.)

Brenton, Edward Pelham, *The Naval History of Great Britain from the year MDCCLXXXIII to MDCCCXXXVI,* Vol. II (London, 1837).

Brown, Glenn, *History of the U. S. Capitol.* (Washington, 1900.)

Brown, Samuel R., *Authentic History of the Second War of Independence.* (Auburn, N. Y., 1815.)

Butler, Nicholas Murray, *The Effect of the War of 1812 upon the Consolidation of the Union.* (Baltimore, Johns Hopkins University Studies, July, 1887.)

Chamier, Frederick, *Life of a Sailor.* (New York, 1833.)

Clark, Allen C., *Life and Letters of Dolly Madison.* (Washington, 1914.)

Cobbett, William, *Letters on the Late War.* (New York, 1815.)

Congreve, William, *A Concise Account of the Origin and Progress of the Rocket System.* (Dublin, 1817.)

Cresson, William Penn, *James Monroe*. (Chapel Hill, N. C., 1946.)

Cullum, George Washington, *Campaigns of the War of 1812 Against Great Britain*. (New York, 1879.)

Cutler, Carl C., *Queens of the Western Ocean*. (Annapolis, 1961.)

Dallas, Alexander James, *An Exposition of the Causes and Character of the Late War Between the United States and Great Britain*. (Middlebury, Vt., 1815.)

Dallas, George, *A Biographical Memoir of Sir Peter Parker*. (London, 1816.)

Daugherty, Charles Michael, *The Army*. (New York, 1958.)

Davis, Paris M., *An Authentic History of the Late War Between the United States and Great Britain*. (New York, 1836.)

Duncan, John M., *Travels Through Part of the United States and Canada in 1818 and 1819*. (Glasgow, 1823.)

Dundonald, Thomas C., *Autobiography of a Seaman*, Vol. I (London, 1860).

Fay, H. A., *Collection of Official Accounts of Battles Fought by Sea and Land between the Navy and Army of the U. S. and the Navy and Army of Great Britain during the Years 1812, 13, 14, and 15*. (New York, 1817.)

Footner, Hulbert, *Rivers of the Eastern Shore*. (New York, 1944.)

———, *Sailor of Fortune: The Life and Adventures of Commodore Barney, U.S.N.* (New York, 1940.)

Forester, C. S., *Age of Fighting Sail*. (Garden City, N. Y., 1956.)

Fortescue, J. W., *A History of the British Army*. (New York, 1917–20.)

Gay, Sydney Howard, *James Madison*. (Boston, 1885.)

Gilleland, J. C., *History of the Late War Between The United States and Great Britain*. (Baltimore, 1817.)

Gilman, Daniel Colt, *James Monroe*. (Boston, 1883.)

Gleig, George Robert, *The Campaigns of the British Army at Washington and New Orleans in the Years 1814–1815*. (London, 1827.)

Green, Constance McLaughlin, *Washington, Village and Capital, 1800–1878*. (Princeton, 1962.)

Griffith, Thomas W., *Annals of Baltimore*. (Baltimore, 1824.)

Gutheim, Frederick, *The Potomac*. (New York, 1949.)

Hall, Clayton Colman, *Baltimore: Its History and Its People.* (New York, 1912.)

Heitman, Francis B., *Historical Register and Dictionary of the U. S. Army from 1789 to 1903.* (Washington, 1903.)

Hildreth, Richard, *The History of the United States of America.* Second series, Vol. III (New York, 1880).

Holloway, Laura C., *The Ladies of the White House.* (Philadelphia, 1881.)

Holst, Herman Edward von, *The Constitutional and Political History of the United States.* (Chicago, 1876.)

Hurd, Charles, *The White House.* (New York, 1940.)

Hurd, Charles, *Washington Cavalcade.* (New York, 1948.)

Ingersoll, Charles Jared, *Historical Sketch of the Second War Between the U. S. A. and Great Britain.* (Philadelphia, 1849.)

Ingraham, Edward Duncan, *A Sketch of the Events Which Preceded the Capture of Washington by the British.* (Philadelphia, 1849.)

James, William, *Inquiry Into Merits of the Principal Naval Actions Between Great Britain and the U. S.* (Halifax, 1816.)

Jenkins, John S., *Generals of the Last War with Great Britain.* (Auburn, N. Y., 1849.)

Jennings, Paul, *A Colored Man's Reminiscences of James Madison.* (Brooklyn, 1865.)

Knox, Dudley W., *A History of the U. S. Navy.* (New York, 1948.)

Lewis, William Frederick, Ed., *Commodore Joshua Barney.* (Springfield, Mass., 1912.)

Lossing, B. J., Ed., *Harper's Encyclopaedia of U. S. History.* (New York, 1912.)

———, *Our Country.* (New York, 1905.)

———, *Pictorial Field Book of War of 1812.* (New York, 1868.)

Lovell, William Stanhope, *Personal Narrative of Events 1799–1815.* (London, 1879.)

Lucas, C. P., *The Canadian War of 1812.* (Oxford, England, 1906.)

Mahan, Alfred Thayer, *Sea Power in Its Relations to the War of 1812.* (Boston, 1905.)

Mann, James, *Medical Sketches of the Campaigns of 1812, 13, 14.* (Dedham, Mass., 1816.)

Marine, William M., *The British Invasion of Maryland, 1812–15*. (Baltimore, 1913.)

McMaster, John Bach, *History of the People of the U. S.*, Vol. IV (New York, 1895).

Metcalf, Clyde H., *History of the United States Marine Corps*. (New York, 1939.)

Moore, Charles, *Washington, Past and Present*. (New York, 1929.)

Muller, Charles G., *The Proudest Day*. (New York, 1960.)

Napier, Elers, *The Life and Correspondence of Admiral Sir Charles Napier*. (London, 1862.)

The Naval Chronicle for 1814, Vol. XXXIII (London).

O'Connor, T., Ed., *An Impartial and Correct History of the War Between the United States of America and Great Britain*. (New York, 1815.)

Paine, Ralph D., *The Fight for a Free Sea*. (New Haven, 1920.)

——, *Joshua Barney*. (New York, 1924.)

Palmer, T. H., Ed., *The Historical Register of the U. S.* (Philadelphia, 1816.)

Park, Lawrence, *Gilbert Stuart: An Illustrated Descriptive List of His Works*, Vol. II, p. 854. (New York, 1926.)

Paullin, Charles Oscar, *Commodore John Rodgers*. (Cleveland, 1910.)

Peck, Taylor, *Round-Shot to Rockets*. (Annapolis, Md., 1949.)

Perkins, Samuel, *History of the Political and Military Events of the Late War*. (New Haven, 1825.)

Roosevelt, Theodore, *The Naval War of 1812*. (New York, 1901.)

Scharf, J. Thomas, *The Chronicles of Baltimore*. (Baltimore, 1874.)

Schouler, James, *History of the United States Under the Constitution*. (Washington, 1886.)

Scott, James, *Recollections of a Naval Life*. (London, 1834.)

Smith, G. C. Moore, Ed., *Autobiography of Lieut. Gen. Sir Harry Smith*. (London, 1901.)

Smith, Margaret Bayard, *First Forty Years of Washington Society*. (New York, 1906.)

Soley, James Russell, *The Boys of 1812 and Other Naval Heroes*. (Boston, 1887.)

Some Unknown Foreigner, *Inchiquin, the Jesuit's Letters*,

During a Late Residence in the United States of America. (New York, 1810.)

Sonneck, Oscar George Theodore, *The Star Spangled Banner.* (Washington, 1914.)

Stahl, John M., *The Invasion of the City of Washington.* (Argos, Ind., 1918.)

————, *The Battle of Plattsburgh.* (Argos, Ind., 1918.)

Stuart, James, *Stuart's Three Years in North America.* (New York, 1833.)

————, *Refutation of Aspersions on "Stuart's Three Years in North America."* (London, 1834.)

Swanson, Neil H., *The Perilous Fight.* (New York, 1945.)

Thomson, John Lewis, *Historical Sketches of the Late War Between the United States and Great Britain.* (Philadelphia, 1818.)

Tucker, Glenn, *Poltroons and Patriots.* (Indianapolis, 1954.)

Tuckerman, Henry T., *Life of John Pendleton Kennedy.* (New York, 1871.)

Tunis, Edwin, *Weapons.* (Cleveland, 1954.)

Williams, John S., *History of the Invasion and Capture of Washington.* (New York, 1857.)

Williams, Samuel, *Sketches of the War Between the United States and the British Isles.* (Rutland, Vt., 1815.)

Wood, William Charles Henry, Ed., *Select British Documents of the Canadian War of 1812.* (Toronto, 1920–28.)

INDEX